MW01027481

Presented to:

_____

From:

_____

Date:

_____

LET'S ALL MAKE THE
DAY COUNT

LET'S ALL MAKE THE
DAY COUNT

THE EVERYDAY WISDOM OF CHARLIE DANIELS

CHARLIE
DANIELS

THOMAS NELSON
Since 1798

Published in Nashville, Tennessee, by Thomas Nelson. Thomas Nelson is a registered trademark of HarperCollins Christian Publishing, Inc.

Published in association with the literary agency of WTA Services, LLC, Franklin, TN.

Thomas Nelson titles may be purchased in bulk for educational, business, fund-raising, or sales promotional use. For information, please e-mail SpecialMarkets@ThomasNelson.com.

Unless otherwise noted, Scripture quotations are taken from the Holy Bible, New International Version®, NIV®. Copyright © 1973, 1978, 1984, 2011 by Biblica, Inc.® Used by permission of Zondervan. All rights reserved worldwide. www.zondervan.com. The "NIV" and "New International Version" are trademarks registered in the United States Patent and Trademark Office by Biblica, Inc.®

Scripture quotations marked AMP are from the Amplified® Bible. Copyright © 1954, 1958, 1962, 1964, 1965, 1987 by The Lockman Foundation. Used by permission. (www.Lockman.org)

Scripture quotations marked CEV are from the Contemporary English Version. Copyright © 1991, 1992, 1995 by American Bible Society. Used by permission.

Scripture quotations marked ESV are from the ESV® Bible (The Holy Bible, English Standard Version®). Copyright © 2001 by Crossway, a publishing ministry of Good News Publishers. Used by permission. All rights reserved.

Scripture quotations marked GNT are from the Good News Translation in Today's English Version—Second Edition. Copyright 1992 by American Bible Society. Used by permission.

Scripture quotations marked HCSB are from the Holman Christian Standard Bible®. Copyright © 1999, 2000, 2002, 2003, 2009 by Holman Bible Publishers. Used by permission. HCSB® is a federally registered trademark of Holman Bible Publishers.

Scripture quotations marked KJV are from the King James Version. Public domain.

Scripture quotations marked MEV are from the Modern English Version. Copyright © 2014 by Military Bible Association. Used by permission. All rights reserved.

Scripture quotations marked NASB are from New American Standard Bible®. Copyright © 1960, 1962, 1963, 1968, 1971, 1972, 1973, 1975, 1977, 1995 by The Lockman Foundation. Used by permission. (www.Lockman.org)

Scripture quotations marked NCV are from the New Century Version®. © 2005 by Thomas Nelson. Used by permission. All rights reserved.

Scripture quotations marked NKJV are from the New King James Version®. © 1982 by Thomas Nelson. Used by permission. All rights reserved.

Scripture quotations marked NLT are from the *Holy Bible*, New Living Translation. © 1996, 2004, 2007, 2013, 2015 by Tyndale House Foundation. Used by permission of Tyndale House Publishers, Inc., Carol Stream, Illinois 60188. All rights reserved.

Scripture quotations marked TLB are from The Living Bible. Copyright © 1971. Used by permission of Tyndale House Publishers, Inc., Carol Stream, Illinois 60188. All rights reserved.

Scripture quotations marked THE VOICE are from The Voice™. © 2012 by Ecclesia Bible Society. Used by permission. All rights reserved. Note: Italics in quotations from The Voice are used to "indicate words not directly tied to the dynamic translation of the original language" but that "bring out the nuance of the original, assist in completing ideas, and . . . provide readers with information that would have been obvious to the original audience" (The Voice, preface).

Any Internet addresses, phone numbers, or company or product information printed in this book are offered as a resource and are not intended in any way to be or to imply an endorsement by Thomas Nelson, nor does Thomas Nelson vouch for the existence, content, or services of these sites, phone numbers, companies, or products beyond the life of this book.

ISBN 978-1-4003-1517-8 (eBook)

Library of Congress Cataloging-in-Publication Data

ISBN 978-1-4003-1488-1 (HC)

Printed in the United States of America

18 19 20 21 22 LSC 10 9 8 7 6 5 4 3 2 1

"Hazel and me dedicate this book to the center of our lives, our son Charles William Daniels. We thought we had our lives figured out until you came along and kicked it all up another notch. What a joy, what a pleasure, what a blessing you have been, and our love for you knows no bounds."

—CHARLIE DANIELS

Let the words of my mouth, and the meditation of my heart, be acceptable in thy sight, O LORD, my strength, and my redeemer.

—PSALM 19:14 KJV

CONTENTS

CONTENTS

INTRODUCTION

For the last five years or so I have posted a daily morning feature on my social media I call "Let's All Make the Day Count."

It's a line or so of personal philosophy, advice, encouragement, or humor that I feel can be a good thought to start the day. Though I occasionally dredge up some old folk saying that I've heard somewhere along the way, most of them are original, and by the grace of God, I come up with them on the spur of the moment.

This book is a collection of one hundred such morning thoughts—each expanded with personal experience or some discovery I've made or lesson I've learned by observing the actions of other people and other situations.

I am a storyteller by nature and profession, as I have spent the last sixty years of my life writing songs about fictional characters and having my way with their actions and outcomes. But this undertaking is different, as it deals mostly with real people and real experiences, so the points I'm trying to make and the lessons imparted are much more important and profound.

I have leaned heavily on my personal journey and the times I've knocked my head against various walls through the years while learning life's lessons.

I've excerpted segments of my highest and lowest times, my most devastating defeats and most rewarding victories, and how I've come to truly value making the day count, every single day.

It is my desire for this collection of my thoughts to be uplifting and encouraging, instilling confidence in an "if I can do it anybody can" and "it's not how many times we stumble but how many times we get back up" sort of way.

At any rate I sincerely hope you will enjoy this little book and that you will be encouraged to make the day count.

LET'S ALL
MAKE THE DAY
COUNT.

1

NEW BEGINNINGS

"See, I am doing a new thing!
Now it springs up; do you not perceive it?
I am making a way in the wilderness
and streams in the wasteland."
—ISAIAH 43:19

In 2011, our barn at Twin Pines Ranch burned to the ground. We lost both of our tractors, both ranch pickups, and seven of our best horses, including a stallion that carried a bloodline we had been working with for almost twenty years.

When we first built our house in 1979, I met with the builder and told him what I wanted: a big barn with several stalls, a hay loft, and an oversized, lighted stall—where we could keep watch of our mares when they gave birth to their foals—along with a shop and an office. When it was finished, we had it all under one roof with an adjacent lighted roping arena. But within just a few hours, it disappeared in a cloud of smoke.

Our ranch manager, Thurman Mullins, was devastated. He had worked for many years building the reputation of Twin Pines and the purity of our breeding stock. Now it was all gone. But the main loss, of course, was the horses and the Twin Pines' bloodline. Most of the other things could be replaced, but it looked as if our bloodline was gone forever.

The morning after the fire, I assured Thurman that we would rebuild. We would make a new beginning. Today a new barn stands on the site. Most of the items we lost in the fire—the tractors, the trucks, and the tack—have been replaced.

And, by the way, we found a stud colt, a magnificent animal, a direct descendant of the stallion we lost. Against all odds, the loss that hurt the most and seemed irreplaceable had been restored.

We named him TP New Beginnings.

If you get up one more time than you get knocked down, you're a winner.

LET'S ALL MAKE THE DAY COUNT.

2

Never Out of Reach

*We live within the shadow of the Almighty,
sheltered by the God who is above all gods.*
—Psalm 91:1 TLB

We were in Iraq, entertaining the troops. We were flying in a Chinook helicopter on our way back to base in Baghdad from doing a show at the soccer stadium in the city of Balad.

Balad had been our third show of the day. Earlier, we had flown to two Forward Operating Bases. FOBs are small remote facilities with limited personnel and strategic missions. They hardly ever see the entertainers who come overseas because most of them only travel to the larger bases, and they're very gratifying shows to do.

The show in Balad had been well received, and we were just winding up a great day. Flying back to our quarters in Baghdad, I heard a *ping*—what I realized later was likely a bullet piercing the outer skin of the helicopter and striking the armor plating under my foot.

Suddenly, bright colored flares started firing, and the pilots jinked the Chinook hard left.

We were under attack! The enemy on the ground was trying to bring us down with small arms fire and a rocket propelled grenade (RPG).

It was over about as fast as it had started. The RPG had missed. The small arms had done no damage, and we landed safely at the base in Baghdad.

To be honest, I thought the whole thing was a maneuver the pilots were doing. I thought it was a practice run on evasive moves, having no idea there were people on the ground trying to kill us.

In fact, I was never really afraid the whole time we were in Iraq. I was being prayed for back home and had made a decision to put my safety in the hands of God.

Actually, it's always in the hands of God anyway.

Trust in the One who is able to protect you in all circumstances.

LET'S ALL MAKE THE DAY COUNT.

3

FAITH AND REALITY

If God is for us, who can be against us?
—ROMANS 8:31

ack in the seventies, when we were getting started, our foot was barely inside the door of the music industry. We were struggling, and we played our music just about anywhere we could get anybody to listen. Each small victory, receptive crowd, standing ovation, or word of encouragement was savored and converted into confidence to fight another day.

The shows we played were small or we played as an opening act for a larger band. But we were working hard, turning the crowds on and making headway, and our aspirations for the future were bright, to say the least.

Then something that could have been very discouraging happened. One of the biggest, most famous and influential concert promoters in the world made the statement that the Charlie Daniels Band would never make it. I don't know what prompted him to say such a thing. Maybe it was just an offhanded remark someone had overheard and passed along until it got to the media. But, whatever the reason, it was hurtful and could have been discouraging if I had let it.

What it came down to for me was this—will I let what he thinks he knows override what I know I know? I believed that this band had the potential to have hit records, to draw big concert crowds, and to make an international name for itself. And nobody, no matter how prominent he or she was in the entertainment business, could dissuade me from that opinion.

So I put my head down and carried on. I used both the encouraging words and discouraging words as fuel to keep fighting. My resolve was to take advantage of every opportunity, go the extra mile, and give it my all every time I walked on stage.

I actually got to be friends with that promoter, and I worked for him many times over the years. He even introduced us one night as the "GREAT, GREAT CHARLIE DANIELS BAND."

If you can't get what you want, take what you can get and make what you want out of it.

LET'S ALL MAKE THE DAY COUNT.

4

HASTY WORDS

But no man can tame the tongue. It is a
restless evil, full of deadly poison.
—JAMES 3:8 HCSB

There have been times in the heat of the moment that I have willfully said something hurtful to someone. Something spiteful or mean-spirited was said with the sole intention of inflicting pain or exacting revenge for some real or imagined slight.

After delivering some scathing barb that hits home and has the intended effect of putting the other person in "their place," I feel so remorseful that I can't have any peace or rest until I find that person and apologize.

Even if I had felt justified in my hasty words, after the swelling of pride goes down, the vitriol of anger has cooled, and rational thinking has returned, there is an uneasy feeling that can only be eased by making things right with the person I've unloaded on.

I have to catch myself before my emotions get out of hand enough to let my anger take over and make me do something I'll regret. Sometimes it seems that our tongue has a mind of its own and gets out of sync with our good senses. Controlling it is a full-time job.

Hurtful words are often completely forgiven but seldom ever completely forgotten.

LET'S ALL
MAKE THE DAY
COUNT.

$$5$$

KEEPING WATCH

Be sure you know the condition of your flocks,
give careful attention to your herds.
—PROVERBS 27:23

I don't consider myself to be a great businessman.

I am basically a romantic, a dreamer who prefers to spend his time rhyming lines of lyric. I would rather be pulling together the notes of a new song or composing lines of prose for some project I'm writing than poring over bank accounts and instructions.

I surround myself with people I trust implicitly, people who have been with me for decades. They add the columns, dot the i's, cross the t's, and bring anything out of the ordinary to my attention to make a decision on.

I can find out the overall and current condition of any aspect of my business by making a quick phone call.

It hasn't always been that way. There was a time when things were falling apart business wise. By the time it was brought to my hardheaded attention, it took divine help and drastic measures to correct our situation.

Though I had put too much confidence and trust in someone else's competence and stewardship, I take all the blame. It's too easy to put the culpability on someone else when I could have taken the occasional hour to catch up on what money was coming in and what money was going out.

Because, even though I could not understand the intricate tax codes and the myriad of ever-changing business curriculum, I could have stayed on top of the overall numbers. I should have kept a closer eye on my flocks and herds.

Lesson learned.

Times change. People change.
Keep a close watch on both.

LET'S ALL
MAKE THE DAY
COUNT.

BRING YOUR A GAME

Whatever you do, work at it with all your heart,
as working for the Lord, not for human masters.
—COLOSSIANS 3:23

It's a proven fact that some days we have more to give on our jobs than on other days. But that is never an excuse not to give everything you've got every time you go to work.

In my case, that means writing a song, recording an album, staying in shape on the instruments I play, and above all, maintaining an attitude of thankfulness for being able to make a living in the business I chose above all others.

Some nights you walk on stage full of energy and the notes just roll off your fingers. It all comes so naturally. Sometimes the lyrics explode in your mind like popcorn, and sometimes you get it on the first couple of takes in the recording studio.

But some nights you stand in the wings of the stage praying for the strength to get through the show.

Sometimes you have to slog through the alphabet time

after time to find a word that will rhyme with a lyric line. Other times, it's take after take in the studio to finally hook a performance.

I'm sure everybody's job is that way to one degree or another. Whether you drive nails, operate a computer, or entertain like me, give it all you've got. Take all three strikes every time you come to the plate.

You're going to knock one out of the park once in a while.

Never leave your A game at home. It's a little heavier but always worth the extra weight.

LET'S ALL MAKE THE DAY COUNT.

Going Up—
Coming Down

*The eyes of the arrogant will be humbled
and human pride brought low.*
—Isaiah 2:11

I once knew a man, a talented, driven man, whose work ethic knew no bounds. He went the extra mile and burned the midnight oil in pursuit of success.

And he achieved success—great success—until he was perched near the pinnacle of his profession, with money and accolades coming from many directions.

He was sought after and much respected. The wins just kept on coming, the money kept rolling in, and his prestige and importance kept growing.

But instead of receiving his blessings with humility and gratitude, he became arrogant and self-absorbed. He treated those around him disrespectfully. He flaunted his power and acted as if his judgment superseded all others' and should never be questioned.

He belittled, made fun of, and embarrassed those he considered to be below his intellect and talent level.

He pursued grandiose projects nobody else believed in and spent lavishly trying to find backing for self-indulgent pipe dreams nobody wanted any part of.

Slowly, his fortune and his popularity drained away. The people he had treated badly, many of whom had gone on to prominence, had no interest in helping him.

He died broken and bitter, never understanding why the world no longer had a place for him. I learned a lot from my observations. A little humility goes a long way, and pride truly does go before a fall.

You meet the same people on the way down that you meet on the way up.

LET'S ALL
MAKE THE DAY
COUNT.

8

THE WHOLE TRUTH

*"Then you will know the truth, and
the truth will set you free."*
—JOHN 8:32

There's a reason the oath you take when you testify in court demands you to tell the *whole* truth, because anything less is not the truth at all.

In today's world, the information we receive from media, politicians, and the business world is so often only half the truth—smoke and mirrors. They are sleight of hand statements designed to mask elements of an agenda, a piece of legislation, or a product that would give the public a look at the whole picture instead of focusing on the part of the iceberg that is below the waterline.

Deception, to one degree or another, has become the way of the world it seems. Polls say that trust for politicians and the media is at an all-time low. When I was younger, I admit I took refuge in a lie more than once. I found out the hard way about the tangled web we weave when we stray from the truth. And it starts to develop the instant an untruth leaves your mouth and grows in proportion to the extent you're willing to go to cover up the original lie you told.

"The check is in the mail" can turn into a convoluted game of cat and mouse—lost in the mail, returned to sender, the dog ate it along with my homework. Anything to postpone the day of reckoning when you finally have to admit you've been lying and wish you'd just told the truth to begin with.

I speak from experience and paid a price for my repentance.

It's always best to tell the whole truth to start with, no matter what the ramifications may be.

It takes years of truth and honesty to build trust, but only one act of betrayal to tear it to shreds.

LET'S ALL
MAKE THE DAY
COUNT.

JUMPING THE GUN

Even in old age they will still produce fruit;
they will remain vital and green.
—PSALM 92:14 NLT

I think that one of the worst things to happen to the American workforce is the mandatory retirement age implemented by many companies.

Now, don't get me wrong: I have absolutely nothing against any hardworking folks who want to hang it up at sixty-five and spend the rest of their days on a golf course or in a bass rig. But, I think if the person is in good health, the retirement should be elective, not compulsory.

I have known some people who were forced to retire at sixty-five who were at the very zenith of their game. With forty years of experience and savvy under their belts, they are turned out to pasture.

Fortunately, I am self-employed, which is a good thing.

The years since my sixty-fifth birthday have been innovative and productive and I have absolutely no designs for retiring.

Forcing a productive person to retire just because of age is a fallacy, and it's a shame to waste such a valuable resource. I understand the reasoning that prevailed when the policy was instituted—when life expectancy was around sixty-one. Their peak productive years were considered to be well behind them. If they were to have any retirement time at all, it was, for all practical purposes, now or never.

Technological advances and modern medicine have vastly increased life expectancy and extended peak years of productivity. So many times, the kind of wisdom and savvy that can only be acquired through firsthand experience of changing times and significant events is stifled and cut off by an employee reaching an arbitrary age. It deprives the company they have served for many years of their hard-earned expertise. People are not automatons. Each individual is different and should be evaluated by talent and attitude, not by age.

*Experience is knowledge
earned in any arena.*

LET'S ALL
MAKE THE DAY
COUNT.

NEVER LET IT GO

"For the revelation awaits an appointed time;
it speaks of the end
and will not prove false.
Though it linger, wait for it;
it will certainly come
and will not delay."

—HABAKKUK 2:3

I am an impatient person when it comes to getting work finished, but there are times when it's necessary to be patient and put an unfinished project aside and let nature take its course.

The old adage "an idea whose time has come" is not only a truism but very applicable to my creative process.

I have held bits and pieces of songs in my head for as long as fourteen years, never able to put them together until, one day, a new thought pops. I pull out the old snatches of melody or lyrics, and, bingo, you've got a thing happening.

I have learned never to discard any good idea, no matter how brief or disjointed it may seem at the time. There will always be a place, at some time in the future, for a truly good idea.

I was sitting on a city bus in El Paso, Texas, in 1962 and had an idea for a song about the Mexican bandit Pancho Villa. I liked the idea a lot but could never get past the first couple of verses. In 1976 I began a song about Billy the Kid. I pulled out the verses I had written fourteen years before about Pancho Villa, made a few adjustments, and, holla, a new song was born.

Hold on to your dreams, your solid ideas, and be on the lookout for the right time to bring them to fruition.

LET'S ALL
MAKE THE DAY
COUNT.

ONE KNOCK

*To every thing there is a season, and a time
to every purpose under the heaven.*
—ECCLESIASTES 3:1 KJV

I n 1967 Bob Johnston, who had just taken over as head of
Columbia Records in Nashville, called me out of the clear
blue sky and asked me if I'd like to move to Music City.

It would mean making a living in one of the most musically competitive towns in the country. It would mean moving
a wife and a two-year-old baby to strange surroundings where
we knew practically nobody and starting all over again.

I talked it over with my wife, and it took her all of about
two minutes to agree with me. Regardless of the obvious
obstacles, we knew we should make the move. We heard the
gentle knock of opportunity and heeded it.

We hit Music City with a twenty-dollar bill and the
clutch burned out on our car.

Our time in Nashville has been a wild and wonderful ride—challenging, exciting, and fulfilling.

We made the move over fifty years ago, and I've never regretted listening to the barely audible voice of opportunity on that day in 1967. I don't even want to think about what would have happened had I not. I've had occasions in my life when a fleeting opportunity has been briefly within my grasp, and if I was not perceptive enough to take advantage, it moved along to knock gently on another door.

Opportunity never lingers; she knocks once, will swiftly move along, and is seldom caught from behind.

LET'S ALL
MAKE THE DAY
COUNT.

12

EXCUSES AND
COMPLAINTS

Do all things without murmurings and disputings.
—PHILIPPIANS 2:14 KJV

There was a time in my life when I had an excuse for practically every shortcoming I owned. Usually it was a way of blaming something or someone else.

And I complained about everything that displeased me.

In other words, I was not willing to take responsibility for my own actions. It was just like saying that everything is completely out of your control, and that you'll have to spend your life being blown here and there by any wind that comes along.

It is an immature and petulant attitude. You soon have to admit that not doing your homework assignment was not because "you ran out of notebook paper," or you didn't hoe the garden because, "you couldn't find the hoe," or you made bad grades because "your teacher didn't like you."

Telling everybody working in a 100-degree tobacco field that it's hot over and over when they already know it and are going through the same thing you are is a waste of time and irritating to those who have to listen.

But when you enter the workplace and real responsibilities fall on your shoulders, where excuses don't cut it and complaints fall on deaf ears, where the competition is tough and not meeting deadlines means a one-way trip back to the farm, reality sets in. You grow up in a hurry or sit on the wayside and watch the rest of the world march off and leave you behind.

Making bogus excuses is lying, and complaining is just your way of saying that you want everybody else to be as miserable as you are.

LET'S ALL MAKE THE DAY COUNT.

---- *13* ----

HOW BAD DO
YOU WANT IT?

Diligent hands will rule.
—PROVERBS 12:24

D o we get back what we put out? Absolutely.

Sometimes we look at successful people and wonder, *Why them? Why not me? Why should they have all the luck?*

Actually, luck has very little to do with it. We are usually looking at the tip of a very large iceberg; the years of hard work and sacrifice are hidden below the waterline.

Usually, he or she is the first one to get there and the last one to leave. They have a let-me-do-it, go-the-extra-mile, burn-the-midnight-oil, and never-give-up attitude applied to endless hours of extra effort that separates the successful from the rest.

The athletes we admire have spent their lives in arduous physical training. The musicians we love to hear have spent countless hours playing scales and practicing on their instruments. Eugene Fodor, one of the world's finest classical violinists, told me that when he was playing concerts he practiced six hours a day.

Stevie Ray Vaughan played his guitar until his fingertips began to shred, applied some liquid skin, and continued to practice until he was the premier blues guitarist of his generation.

Everything comes with a price.

There's an old saying, "If you want to run with the big dogs, you've got to get off the porch."

Success is shaped like a pyramid with a lot of room at the bottom. But the closer to the top you get, the smaller it gets.

LET'S ALL
MAKE THE DAY
COUNT.

14

DOING A DAY'S WORK TODAY

Don't put it off; do it now!
Don't rest until you do.
—PROVERBS 6:4 NLT

Procrastination can be bad enough when it only involves the little mundane things—everyday tasks like cutting the grass. But the penalties for that are only an unkempt yard and an irritated wife. When applied to your livelihood, procrastination is like a snowball. It can start out very small, but the further it's allowed to roll, the bigger and more cumbersome it becomes.

When we were on major record labels, they wanted a new album every year. Now, that doesn't sound like a particularly hard task. But when you take into consideration that we wrote our own material and it entailed ten new songs every twelve months, it takes on a little more gravity.

I've always worked a little different than most song-writers. I liked to have the band around so I could instantly hear the parts they would play as I came up with them. The upshot was that we would create a bevy of new songs, complete with musical arrangements and instrumental breaks, without so much as a line of lyric, and sometimes without a title.

So it was my responsibility to do the lyrics. Which, when you have several sets of words to write and a time line looming over your head, can seem a little intimidating. I always delivered on time, but I procrastinated. I was fortunate I was always able to get done in time. But in so many instances, if you leave today's work until tomorrow, you'll probably never really get caught up. You've just combined today's problems with tomorrow's. This means you won't have the time to devote full attention to either.

The old aphorism about not putting off until tomorrow what you can do today is just common sense.

LET'S ALL MAKE THE DAY COUNT.

15

BUCKING THE ODDS

If you falter in a time of trouble,
how small is your strength!
—PROVERBS 24:10

The pages of history are loaded with those who were bold enough to go against the odds even to the point that what they were attempting at the time was counter to any kind of rational thought. They were considered "tetched" and a prime target of ridicule.

When God told Noah to build the ark to survive the flood to come, it had never rained. Can you imagine Noah trying to explain the gigantic structure and its purpose to his contemporaries? I'm sure they would have tried to commit him to the funny farm if they had had such a thing in that time.

And if building the ark was not enough, he went out and started collecting a huge herd of animals and put them on board the monstrosity after he built it.

But when Noah and his family finished their work, went on board, closed the door, and the rain began to fall, nobody was laughing. Only eight people—Noah, his wife, his three sons and their wives—escaped the flood.

Talk about going against the odds. Noah went against every other person on earth. He refused to succumb to the derision and ridicule of the majority. Instead, he put his head down and did what God had told him to do.

Do you have something that only you believe in? Are you willing to risk failure and ridicule to bring it forth, no matter what everybody else thinks?

Well, go ahead and buck the odds. If it doesn't work the first time, try again with that dream or a new one.

Listening to the crowd has killed many a good idea.

Opinions are common; everybody has one. When it comes to what you're capable of, nobody's opinion is as important as your own.

LET'S ALL MAKE THE DAY COUNT.

16

THOUGHTS ARE THINGS

If anything is excellent or praiseworthy—
think about such things.
—PHILIPPIANS 4:8

The dictionary defines *thought* as the action of thinking. This is a very broad and inclusive definition that nobody can argue with.

But thoughts are not merely the firing of electric impulses in the brain. Thoughts are actually things. While intangible and untouchable, thoughts are the beginning of every grandiose scheme mankind has ever dared to attempt.

From the wheel to mind-boggling, ever-changing technology, it all starts as a single thought in the brains of human beings.

The ability to think, reason, and plan comes to us from our Creator, who has endowed us with the ability to do great good, and conversely, great evil.

It all begins with the thoughts we choose to devote our intellect to.

Negative thinking, imagining revenge, plotting less-than-honest endeavors, dwelling on forbidden pleasures, and all such things can be fascinating and elicit a dark satisfaction. But they ultimately take away from creativity and production, play havoc with your attention span, and if not dealt with, can dominate your whole thought process.

It's a never-ending thing, this culling of thoughts—an ongoing procedure of recognizing and admitting to yourself what is constructive or destructive and making a conscious effort to make the right choices.

It's not an easy job, but with God's help it can be done.

The thoughts you allow yourself to think will govern the kind of person you will become.

LET'S ALL
MAKE THE DAY
COUNT.

17

KEEP ON KNOCKING

*"Ask and it will be given to you; seek and you will
find; knock and the door will be opened to you."*
—MATTHEW 7:7

Dreams are only wistful thoughts until they are combined
with action. Until then, they live only in our minds,
locked behind doors we haven't knocked on yet.

Sometimes following a dream is like jumping off the high
diving board into the deep water and having to learn to swim
all over again.

It can require sacrifice. Doing something we've never
done before. Learning, asking, seeking. Sometimes taking
two steps forward and one step back. But constantly and
unwaveringly moving toward the goal.

I've knocked on a lot of doors in my time, returning again
and again. Even when they refused to budge, I just kept on
knocking, and finally the doors opened.

One of the true desires of my life was to become a member of the Grand Ole Opry.

I played the Opry for years but was never asked to join. It seemed that door would never open for me, but I just kept on knocking. Finally, at the age of seventy-two, I was asked to be a member, and it was one of the biggest honors of my life and absolutely worth all the hard work and waiting it took to get there.

Something that began as what seemed to be an impossible dream in the mind of a Carolina country boy many decades ago came true.

Sometimes knocking is not enough. You've just got to stay with it until you beat the door down.

LET'S ALL MAKE THE DAY COUNT.

18

PRECIOUS WISDOM

Do not forsake wisdom, and she will protect you;
love her, and she will watch over you.
—PROVERBS 4:6

I believe we are born with a certain amount of innate wisdom. It is the kind that develops our natural instincts to
walk, eat, and talk.

But other wisdom can only be learned. And it seems that
some people, like me for instance, can only learn the hard way.

I gained the wisdom that I'm not good with machinery
by cutting off part of a finger and breaking an arm. I'm wise
enough now to avoid close contact with things that have a
bunch of moving parts.

True wisdom usually comes through experience and is
only wisdom if it sticks with you and becomes a part of you
and your decision-making process. Wisdom always involves
truth and honesty and having the courage to admit to yourself that no matter how much something appeals to you, it

may not be good for you. The easiest way is not always the right way.

So much wisdom is just common sense, the humility to be objective about all things, and the willingness to admit when you're wrong.

Live by something I call cowboy logic:
Water never runs uphill.
Two and two is always four.
If there's smoke, there's a fire somewhere.

LET'S ALL
MAKE THE DAY
COUNT.

19

MAKING THE CUT

*Let us not grow weary of doing good, for in due
season we will reap, if we do not give up.*
—GALATIANS 6:9 ESV

It took me a lot of years to discover, or at least admit, that my athletic talent was limited. I was of the opinion that if I practiced hard enough and long enough I could develop the smooth, unhurried motions of the kids who obviously had the natural instincts and ability of an athlete.

When I was around sixteen, the boys club I was a member of formed a softball team to play other sandlot kids' teams in the city. I went out for it and worked hard to secure a position on it. When the roster was announced, I was not on it. In fact, I was the only kid who went out for the team who didn't make the cut.

I was devastated; I didn't understand. I guess it was my introduction into the world of competition. I went out for the football team at Tileston Jr. High the next year. I decided to try out for the center position. That summer before school started, I got with some older kids who taught me some things about playing the position. I worked hard all summer, and when the school year came, I walked into the tryouts prepared and confident.

I played first-string center for Tileston that year. It was not because I had developed any more athletic ability, but because I went out for a position I was able to play and that was within my limited talents. I prepared for it, and I wanted it with all my heart.

Competition is a fact of life, and your willingness and ability to meet it will determine how far you'll go in your career. It starts by being brutally honest with yourself about your abilities. Pick the strong points. Prepare and get ready to sweat.

*Don't mind the extra effort. It's a
small price for living your dream.*

LET'S ALL MAKE THE DAY COUNT.

 20

FIRM FOUNDATIONS

"And when the flood arose, the stream beat
vehemently upon that house, and could not
shake it: for it was founded upon a rock."
—LUKE 6:48 KJV

Make the first row you plow straight as an arrow; otherwise, the whole field will be crooked.

This is an old farming adage and so true. If the first row you plow is crooked, the other rows will have to follow in the same pattern, and the whole field will look misshapen and haphazard. No farmer worth his salt is willing to let that happen.

John Boylan, the record producer we had the most success with, had a saying, "No amount of overdubbing can fix a bad track."

Meaning that, if the rhythm track, the foundation, bass, drums, etc. is flawed, no matter how brilliant the guitar solos or how great the vocals are, the foundation is flawed so the whole record will be flawed.

It can become extremely tedious and nerve-racking doing the same song over and over again—like laying down a rhythm track that will be the underlying base and the shoulders the whole song will stand on. But when it's finished and you're listening to the playback, you realize that it was worth every lick.

Doing it until you get it right can be a tough thing, but always, without a doubt, the right thing. Make a firm foundation before you ever start raising the roof.

Our lives are that way too. If we allow ourselves to be poorly educated, develop detrimental habits at a young age, or evolve into a sloppy work ethic, our foundations are built on sand and will not withstand the heavy storms of life.

We should lay our foundations carefully after first seeking solid ground.

Measure twice, cut once.

LET'S ALL
MAKE THE DAY
COUNT.

21

TURN IT LOOSE

Do not let the sun go down on your wrath.
—EPHESIANS 4:26 NKJV

Have you ever taken a grudge to bed with you?

I have, and I never intend to do it again. Sleep and anger make incompatible bedfellows. The anger usually turns to thoughts of getting even and paying back in kind. The plotting can go on until the wee small hours, and when the sun rises, you've accomplished absolutely nothing except depriving yourself of a good night's sleep.

There is a mechanism, a release valve, for you to turn to so that a grudge does not get the best of you. It's called forgiveness.

Forgiveness works like this: you don't have to condone a wrongful act, *but*, if you want to have peace in your life, you do have to forgive it. After all, your thoughts are not really hurting anybody but you. Put aside thoughts of vengeance and harm. Take a deep breath. Forgive. Let it go with the knowledge that it is not your place but God's to make all things right.

Conversely, if you are the offender, it's your place to ask the person you offended for forgiveness. If you do it before the sun goes down, you'll get a much better night's sleep.

Taking ill feelings to bed with you is like trying to sleep with a cactus plant.

Let it go.

Holding on to a grudge is like holding a tiger's tail; eventually it will turn and consume you.

LET'S ALL
MAKE THE DAY
COUNT.

22

SWEAT VERSUS LUCK

Go to the ant, you sluggard;
consider its ways and be wise!
It has no commander,
no overseer or ruler,
yet it stores its provisions in summer
and gathers its food at harvest.
—PROVERBS 6:6–8

Occasionally, somebody will tell me how lucky I've been to have had success at my chosen profession—to have pursued it for sixty years and to still be able to do it at my advanced age.

Actually, if we can substitute the word *blessed* for the word *lucky*, I would agree with every word.

God has indeed blessed me, but luck has nothing to do with it.

While my contemporaries in high school were going to movies and all the other recreational activities teenagers indulge in, I was usually sitting at home trying to figure out a guitar riff or a fiddle lick.

And after I started playing professionally, when folks went home to their families after work at night, I was five hundred miles away from mine, making a living and trying to further my music career.

While others had a regular paycheck, if I had one, I made it myself. I had no company with deep pockets to guarantee me that I'd have a job next week.

The point I'm making is that what you see on the surface is only the manifestation of the hard work expended and the sacrifices made to get there. Never judge a book by its cover.

Luck notwithstanding.

The kind of luck you can depend on is the kind you make yourself, and it's found mainly among the industrious.

LET'S ALL
MAKE THE DAY
COUNT.

23

TREASURED WORDS

Gray hair is a crown of splendor;
it is attained in the way of righteousness.
—PROVERBS 16:31

My grandfather, or granddaddy as I called him, was born in 1895 and was a master woodsman.

He could build a house or a boat, plant and harvest a crop, run a trotline, skin a deer, and he had a head full of common sense and know-how.

I learned a lot from my granddaddy and quite a few of the old folks who crossed my path and passed on hard-earned wisdom and practical advice.

I come from a day when people depended on themselves, accepted reality, and dealt with each situation as it came up. Without safety nets or health insurance, they lived in a smaller world. They chose to devote their attention and energy to taking care of the things they were able to handle and leaving the rest to the Lord.

They knew all the shortcuts, the best fishing spots, where a big buck was apt to cross the road, the proper way to fell a tree, or the right spot to dig a well.

Their word was as good as gold. Their counsel was wise and enlightening, and honesty came as naturally as breathing.

Never let gray hair, advanced age, or the fact that an elderly person may be out of touch with the times fool you into thinking there's nothing to be learned from them.

Old dogs are slower, but they know more tricks.

LET'S ALL
MAKE THE DAY
COUNT.

24

UNWANTED ADVICE

The simple believe anything,
but the prudent give thought to their steps.
—PROVERBS 14:15

Do you know folks who consider themselves the world's foremost expert on every subject and give unsolicited advice on any issue that comes up, whether they know anything about it or not?

I think we all know somebody like that. They have the answer to every situation and are all too happy to share it without being asked to do so. And just to be truthful, we're all probably guilty of giving unwelcome advice to one degree or another.

After all, it's one of the biggest temptations.

I am a terrible golfer, but I enjoy the game and play it occasionally. After hitting an awful shot, I am still tempted to instruct the people I'm playing with how to hit theirs—even after proving I don't know what I'm talking about by knocking my ball in the woods or a pond.

"What you ought to do" and "what I would do" are probably two of the most unwelcome phrases known to man, and most times, they are better kept to oneself.

Unsolicited advice is about as welcome as a cloud of mosquitoes.

LET'S ALL
MAKE THE DAY
COUNT.

25

MAKING PEACE

"Blessed are the peacemakers,
for they will be called children of God."
—MATTHEW 5:9

Being a peacemaker does not brand you as some milque-toast softie who is afraid of his own shadow and who tries to placate evil and injustice at any price.

The same Bible that says "blessed are the peacemakers" also tells us that we shouldn't stand by and watch the defenseless be mistreated or let wickedness flourish. Sometimes making peace takes drastic measures.

Ronald Reagan advocated "peace through strength" and built the mightiest military the planet had ever known. He stood ready to use it and stared down the Russians. It resulted in the tearing down of the Berlin Wall and the end of the Cold War.

The Prince of Peace will return to the earth with a mighty army to destroy all evil and create real peace—undaunted by the satanic forces that have plagued mankind since the garden of Eden.

On a person-to-person level, I believe that God wants us to help mediate arguments and disagreements when the occasion presents itself. We should maintain peace in our own relationships and promote peaceful solutions whenever we can.

We will only know true and unending peace when we come into the presence of our Creator. Until then, I believe that He wants us to be peacemakers, whatever that entails.

*First of all, make
peace with yourself.*

LET'S ALL
MAKE THE DAY
COUNT.

26

CLOSE CALL IN
THE ROCKIES

*And we know that all things work together
for good to them that love God.*
—ROMANS 8:28 KJV

We were fifteen miles up a snowmobile trail in the beautiful Colorado backcountry, running in perfect powder, and enjoying the views you can only find in the Rocky Mountains when my left hand started feeling numb.

I also noticed a numbness in my left foot and the left side of my jaw, and I knew something out of the ordinary was happening. I told my friends who were riding along with me that I needed to head back down to the trailhead. It was the longest fifteen miles of my life coming down off that mountain, feeling almost certain I was having a stroke.

Fortunately, we were on the same side of Durango, Colorado, as Mercy Hospital. We could have easily been fifty miles in another direction, so the trip to the emergency room was short. I was immediately given a scan that confirmed I was having a stroke caused by a blood clot on the right side of my brain. I was given a shot of tPA to dissolve it. To be effective the shot needs to be administered within a set amount of time after the stroke begins. I had only fifteen or twenty minutes left by the time I got to the emergency room and was diagnosed.

A medically equipped plane was available. They took me to Swedish Medical Center in Denver, one of the finest stroke hospitals in the country. I was treated and released in two days with little permanent damage from the stroke. Here's the kicker: Mercy Regional Medical Center in Durango had only stocked the clot buster tPA in their pharmacy three months prior. Had they not had it, I could not have gotten it in time to limit the damage. Angels watching? Indeed!

*Don't let fear of the unknown
hinder the way you live your life.
Remember, you're in good hands.*

LET'S ALL
MAKE THE DAY
COUNT.

27

PERSEVERANCE

Be joyful in hope, patient in
affliction, faithful in prayer.
—ROMANS 12:12

I read a true story once about a man who found a location where he believed with all his heart a gold deposit was located. But after digging and digging without finding anything, he got discouraged and quit, so someone else acquired the claim.

The new owner dug down one more foot and found a rich vein of gold. The original owner had given up a mere twelve inches from the dream he'd pursued so hard.

Conversely, Thomas Edison tried ten thousand different filaments for his first light bulb before he found tungsten. He refused to give up on his dream.

The pages of human history are filled with stories of those who tried and tried again—refusing to give up on a vision, experiencing failure after failure, persevering through ridicule, or burning through fortunes. They never took their eyes off the goal. Until one day, the dream was realized and all the disappointment fell away like morning mist.

And where would the world be without such people—the adventurous sailors who discovered new continents, the stubborn scientists who spent decades finding cures for our most dreaded diseases, the intrepid inventors who brought us everything from the cotton gin to atomic power.

Well, you may not find a new land or perfect a cure for cancer, but you surely have aspirations. Don't give up on your dream. If you believe in it, go for it. If you find something you believe in with all your heart, get after it!

It's worth chasing until you can hold it in your hand.

Progress is made by continuously putting one foot in front of the other to constantly move toward a goal.

LET'S ALL MAKE THE DAY COUNT.

28

NASTY HABIT

*No temptation has overtaken you that is not
common to man. God is faithful, and he will
not let you be tempted beyond your ability.*
—1 CORINTHIANS 10:13 ESV

I started smoking in my very early teens. By the time I
reached my late twenties, I was smoking four to five packs
of cigarettes a day.

Every cold I had was exacerbated by the massive amount
of smoke I was putting into my lungs. It got to the point that
every slight infection became a chronic bout of sore throats,
coughing, stuffy head and chest, and an overall flu-like
feeling.

I got up one morning in 1968, after years of blaming my
condition on anything but my nicotine habit, and I finally
admitted to myself that my problem was the eighty to one
hundred cigarettes I was smoking each day. I made the bold
statement, "I will never smoke another cigarette."

Later in the morning when my lungs started loosening up and my breathing got easier, I truly regretted my statement. I wanted to light up worse than anything else I could think of. I constantly reached into my shirt pocket for the pack of smokes that, after fifteen years, wasn't there anymore.

But a vow is a vow. I stuck it out through the rabid craving and, in about three weeks, it was all over. My appetite for cigarettes was gone, and the habit was broken.

I have not smoked another cigarette since that morning in 1968. What a blessing!

You can overcome a nasty habit one minute, one step, one day at a time, facing down each trial as it appears.

LET'S ALL
MAKE THE DAY
COUNT.

29

WORDS WITH MEANING

Pleasant words are a honeycomb,
sweet to the soul and healing to the bones.
—PROVERBS 16:24 NASB

I never let a day go by without telling my wife that I love her, usually several times a day. Not that she doesn't already know it, because we've been married for fifty-four years. Despite the fact that I'm eighty-two and she's seventy-five, we hug a lot, hold hands, snuggle, and constantly speak endearments to each other.

Many days, except for the three hours my on-the-road concert schedule demands, we are together twenty-four hours and never tire of each other's company.

Our son, Charlie, is in his fifties, and he always hugs his mother and me every time he comes to our house. Even at the end of a telephone conversation, we always say, "I love you." I can't remember a time in my childhood when greeting kinfolk and friends of the family didn't involve a hug. It was just something you did naturally, just a part of saying hello.

I am of the opinion that hugs and words of affection are healing; I don't think there's enough of either in today's society.

I hug my employees if I haven't seen them for a while. I even hug someone I'm meeting for the first time if it seems fitting.

As long as I live, my little corner of the world will always be an affectionate place.

---

*An apt word and a good hug can
make up for a lot of ill feelings.*

LET'S ALL
MAKE THE DAY
COUNT.

3o

THE SENSE OF A GOOSE

Two are better than one, because they have a good
reward for their toil. For if they fall, one will lift
up his fellow. But woe to him who is alone when
he falls and has not another to lift him up!
—ECCLESIASTES 4:9–10 ESV

When you see a flight of geese overhead, if they are traveling for any extended distance, they will be flying in a V-formation. You'll also notice a single goose in the lead and the others spread out in the V following the leader.

This is done for aerodynamics, similar to the way NASCAR racers draft off the car in front of them. The geese do much the same thing flying beak to tail, taking some of the air resistance off each other.

When the lead goose gets tired, he drops back. A fresh goose takes his place, and the flight goes on.

If one of the geese in the flight gets sick or, for whatever reason, has to go down to the ground, two other geese drop out of the formation. They go to the ground with the sick bird and stay until it gets better or dies. Pending the outcome, they return to the air and try to catch up with their flight.

If they are too far behind to catch up, they'll join the formation of another flight and continue on.

Geese mate for life. Sensible bunch.

---

*Lift your light high so that
those whose lights are dimming
may share in its glow.*

LET'S ALL
MAKE THE DAY
COUNT.

WRONG TURNS

Walk with the wise and become wise,
for a companion of fools suffers harm.
—PROVERBS 13:20

When you're young, it's natural to want to fit in with the crowd, to go along with the collective will of the people you consider cool. Peer pressure is relentless, and it hurts to be a square peg. To be called a chicken or a dolt spoils all the fun.

I went along with the crowd when I was young—skipping school, sneaking cigarettes and such. But, when I threw a handful of rocks through the windows of William Hooper Elementary School in Wilmington, North Carolina, one summer afternoon and a city policeman came to see me about it, I realized that I could get into the kind of trouble that could land me in detention. That scared the daylights out of me. It was a good lesson to learn.

I thought I'd gotten away with breaking out the windows.

I didn't think anybody who would snitch on me had seen it. And just to be truthful, at that age, I couldn't see it as a big deal. After all, it was just broken panes of glass in a school that was closed down for the summer.

But the visit from the police officer was a real eye-opener. There he was, in uniform, asking me questions about what I'd done. Without batting an eye I came clean. Lying never even crossed my mind, although I didn't know what owning up would get me into. Like most boys that age, I was terrified of "reformatory school" as they called it in those days. But putting a good scare into me was probably all the policeman intended to do, and if that was the case, he achieved his goal.

Although I can't claim that I lived a completely mischief-free life from then on, I avoided the weightier stuff like the plague. When the crowd I was with headed in that direction, I went my own way.

Going along with the crowd may lead to places you don't want to go.

Let's All Make the Day Count.

32

WORK ETHIC

May the favor of the Lord our God rest on us;
establish the work of our hands for us—
yes, establish the work of our hands.
—PSALM 90:17

The basics of my work ethic were not gained by playing musical instruments and singing.

They were birthed in a white, hot, bright, leaf-tobacco field, the logging woods, the humid yards of a creosote plant, and working in a factory. And I wouldn't trade anything for the experience.

I learned to work with plows, chain saws, cant hooks, hoes, and axes. I sweated it out with men who had no aspirations to do anything else than what they were doing. I had the opportunity to witness men content with their lot in life and committed to giving a day's work for a day's pay. All this laid the ground work for how I would view my music career when the time came.

And though it's more mental than physical, applying the same "if I don't do it, it won't get done; gather the crop when it's ripe; whatever it takes" approach has served me well.

I wish all young people could spend a period of time doing heavy manual labor. It would help develop empathy, responsibility, and a strong work ethic.

Work ethic isn't something you're born with; you must earn it.

LET'S ALL
MAKE THE DAY
COUNT.

—— *33* ——

GO FOR IT

*"But as for you, be strong and do not give
up, for your work will be rewarded."*
—2 CHRONICLES 15:7

You feel like you deserve a promotion or a raise, but you won't ask because you're afraid they'll say no.

You feel the need to make a major move in your life, maybe by changing jobs or moving to a new location. You know there are opportunities out there for you, but you're afraid to get out of your comfort zone and seek them out.

You have an innovative idea, but you're afraid to approach the people who can help you and present it. You're afraid of being rejected or laughed at.

And the truth of the matter is that you may well be told no, make the wrong move or job change, or be ridiculed or laughed at when you show your idea to someone.

I have been laughed at, have been ridiculed, and have even made a bunch of wrong business decisions. But, taking no for an answer or giving up on an idea I believe in just because somebody else doesn't like it, has not been an option for me.

There's an old saying that I very much ascribe to. When somebody says, "You can't do that," my response is, "Well, I wouldn't feel right if I didn't try." The truth is that you never know what you can accomplish until you give it your best shot.

Please don't get me wrong, I don't blame anybody for playing it safe, staying close to shore, or only betting on the sure thing if that's what it takes to make them feel secure. But how many people in their advanced age sit and dream about the time in their youth they had the chance to "leave town with the circus" and decided to stay home?

If you don't believe in yourself, nobody else will. People who believe in themselves are willing to take chances.

LET'S ALL MAKE THE DAY COUNT.

34

REAL RESPECT AND FALSE PRIDE

"Blessed are the meek, for they shall inherit the earth."
—MATTHEW 5:5 ESV

Many people in the public eye are extremely image-conscious. They pay public relations firms thousands of dollars a year to help them project the personality and characteristics they want the public to perceive them as having.

Many times the images are true reflections. They are admired by the like-minded segment of the public as being an outdoorsman, a sports enthusiast, or one with certain political and social beliefs, or whatever the image may be.

However, if they are found to be a charlatan who appears to be one thing and is really another and word spreads, the admiration wanes.

I have met people that, judging by their public persona, I had a favorable preconceived opinion of, only to find out they were impatient, snobbish, or downright rude. I never felt the same way about that person again, not a feeling of abhorrence but of disappointment.

Presenting yourself to be something you're not, claiming beliefs you have no conviction of, public humility and private arrogance, eventually catches up with those who travel that fickle path.

There's a lot to be said for just being yourself, privately *and* publicly.

Trying to be someone other than who you really are is an exercise in futility.

LET'S ALL MAKE THE DAY COUNT.

35

AS IF THERE'S
NO TOMORROW

This is the day that the LORD has made;
let us rejoice and be glad in it.
—PSALM 118:24 ESV

A day is a unique thing. It is a twenty-four-hour segment of time that will never be repeated—a period of time when things will happen that will never happen again; a day when human beings will be born and die, and when relationships will be formed or shattered. The date will never appear again.

I have had friends who were sick, and I knew they were getting close to the end. I put off going to see them until it was too late.

I've missed timely opportunities, failed to meet deadlines, blown appointments, and had a thousand other shortcomings for the simple reason that I forgot about the importance of *today*. There will be opportunities today that may never come again.

I remember a night a few years ago when we were traveling across the northern part of the country in our bus. My wife and I had gone to bed, and our driver rang the intercom to tell us that the Northern Lights were visible. Of course, we got up and went to the front of the bus and enjoyed the spectacle, which could very well have been a once-in-a-lifetime opportunity.

If you look around, every day is special in some way.

There is no day like today. It will never return, rewind, or replay. It comes once with all its unique opportunities and one-of-a-kind attributes. Any "today" could be the last one we'll ever see.

Life has no dress rehearsal.
When the curtain goes up,
it's always the main event.

LET'S ALL
MAKE THE DAY
COUNT.

36

SHORTCUTS
AND SETBACKS

Good planning and hard work lead to prosperity,
but hasty shortcuts lead to poverty.
—PROVERBS 21:5 NLT

Have you ever tried to save some time by taking a shortcut? Maybe you found your way blocked by a closed road or a traffic jam and ended up having to travel twice as far as you would have, had you stuck to the regular route from the get-go.

Or have you ever changed the TV to the other football game with only a few seconds left on the game clock, to later find out that the play of the season took place after you'd left the channel? Now you're forever relegated to watching a taped replay.

Have you ever decided to take the scenic route, only to find yourself stuck on tiny two-lane roads with no way to get back to the interstate without traveling another fifty miles?

In my business, shortcuts don't usually work out too well. If you hurry through rehearsal, don't run the new material enough, and go on stage not fully prepared, you'll find yourself terrified while standing in front of thousands of people because you can't remember the first words to the next verse.

Getting there for sure is much more important than getting there quickly.

Shortcuts that are not well-thought-out can become lengthy detours.

LET'S ALL
MAKE THE DAY
COUNT.

37

THE COMPANY WE KEEP

*"Your eyes light up your inward being. A pure eye
lets sunshine into your soul. A lustful eye shuts
out the light and plunges you into darkness."*
—MATTHEW 6:22–23 TLB

It is said that we are judged by the company we keep. While
I do not question the validity of that statement, I think the
implications are pretty broad. In business or other purposes,
most of us are forced to be around people and groups we certainly have no desire to be assimilated into.

It's only when you begin to emulate these people, become
part of their crowd, and do the things they do that the trouble
starts.

How many serious drug habits have been started by running with the wrong crowd? Practically 100 percent! But, in
so many cases, nobody forces someone to try it the first time.
The Bible says that the eye is the light of the body. If that light
is darkness, how deep that darkness can be.

It took me a long time to understand this passage of Scripture. I comprehend it to mean that when we continue to let darkness into our eyes it has a cumulative effect, and before long, it tries to control us.

How many serious pornography habits began with leaving certain TV channels on just a little too long until it becomes regular watching? But nobody stops you from changing channels.

What we willingly let into our consciousness will eventually determine the course of our lives. Good and evil are both perceived by the same eye. But what we let in and what we shut out is up to us.

*Guard your eyes, your tongue,
and your temper, and most
everything else will fall into place.*

LET'S ALL MAKE THE DAY COUNT.

38

EMPTY WORDS

Broken promises
are worse than rain clouds
that don't bring rain.
—Proverbs 25:14 cev

In my early twenties, I had a hot little four-piece band. We all worked daytime jobs and played just about anywhere they'd have us at night and on weekends, hoping for that elusive break that could make us full-time musicians.

I don't know how many guys came up to me and told me that our band was capable of great things and that they had the connections to start the ball rolling. Being inexperienced and vulnerable, it always got my hopes up, only to have them disappear in a day or so, taking their fabulous connections with them.

It happened so much that when the real thing finally did come along, through a man who actually did have the ability to help us make a forward move, I lumped him in with the rest of the pretenders and ignored him.

When he left town he promised to call, though I never expected to hear from him again. But true to his word, he did call. He helped get the ball rolling and played a significant part in my early career.

How do you separate the wheat from the chaff when you're dealing with people you're considering seriously associating yourself and your future with?

Look for the promise keeper, the word keeper. Wait for the right enthusiastic, energetic, and honest person to come along before you let that person help pull your wagon, and avoid any other kind.

Promises are cheap. And grandiose expectations are only exciting dreams until there's some meat on the bone.

Even if it's signed and sealed, if it's not delivered, the deal ain't done yet.

LET'S ALL
MAKE THE DAY
COUNT.

39

A TOTALLY UNEXPECTED
BLESSING

*Take delight in the Lord,
and he will give you the desires of your heart.*
—Psalm 37:4

On October 16, 2016, I was given an honor that came completely out of the blue like a lightning bolt. I was inducted into the Country Music Hall of Fame.

I had been told about it several weeks before and my reaction was emotional to say the least. It's an accomplishment that you can only dream about as there is no practical way to go about achieving it. It is strictly decided on by a group of your peers, and you don't even know who they are.

There are only three inductions each year, and to be one of the three is an honor beyond description.

I know in my heart that there are those out there who deserve to be inducted in the Hall of Fame much more than

94

I do. I do not write about my induction to in any way elevate myself but to illustrate the goodness of God.

Although I thought there was a good possibility that I would never be inducted, I will admit that it was a treasured desire of my heart, and God granted it.

As I look back over my eighty-two years, I can see where the hand of God has been so evident in my life. In times of danger, He has protected me. He has lifted me out of financial trouble, given me a wonderful woman to share my life with, and given us a child and grandchildren to love.

And His fingerprints are all over my career. I attribute every good thing that has ever happened to me to Him and His Son Jesus Christ, my Lord and Savior.

Dare to dream, continue to hope, keep your faith front and center, and walk on.

LET'S ALL
MAKE THE DAY
COUNT.

40

YOUR OWN WORLD

Spend time with the wise and you will become wise,
but the friends of fools will suffer.
—PROVERBS 13:20 NCV

Although I'm forced to from time to time, I really dislike getting out of my comfort zone, which has nothing to do with geography. Traveling thousands of miles a year, waking up in a different town every morning, or working on a different stage every night has no bearing on it.

My comfort zone is built around familiarity. I like my own brand of English breakfast tea every morning. I want to play the same guitar and fiddle every show. And most of all, I want to be surrounded by the same people.

I have several employees who have been with me for well over forty years. These are relationships that transcend employer-employee; they are friends whose personal lives I care deeply about.

I am a small-town, rural type of person. Once I asked

a lady who lived in one of the biggest cities in the country, "How can you stand to live in this huge place with all these people?"

She responded with something like, "You just take your area and your friends and you make that your world."

Wise words.

We are all islands in a vast and sometimes intimidating sea of humanity. Yet, surrounded by the things we love and the people we trust, serenity can be found.

Familiar faces in strange places vanish anxiety.

LET'S ALL MAKE THE DAY COUNT.

———— *41* ————

THE LEAST AMONG US

"Truly I tell you, whatever you did for one of the least
of these brothers and sisters of mine, you did for me."
—MATTHEW 25:40

I remember when I was a kid, some people, who considered themselves to be good Christians, looked down on those they considered less virtuous than them. Their condescension was many times biting and acerbic and spoken without the slightest knowledge of how or why the object of their scorn had arrived at the condition they were in.

"He's a drunk."

"She's a streetwalker."

"That family sends their children to school in rags."

How can we know what drives someone to the place of dulling the pain with alcohol? What forces a woman to look for a remedy for unrelenting loneliness? Or how does a family reach the point of poverty?

Are these not the least among us? Did our Lord not tell us that whatever we did for them was like doing it for Him?

Shouldn't we try to help instead of criticize? Should we not begin with a little kindness and understanding? Should we not realize that in the eyes of the Lord, their souls are just as precious as ours?

When we consider ourselves above others, we actually tend to slip several rungs down the ladder.

LET'S ALL MAKE THE DAY COUNT.

42

QUESTIONABLE CHOICES

Discretion will protect you,
and understanding will guard you.
—PROVERBS 2:11

I can remember when I decided to take a hit off a cigarette when the other kids were passing it around. And I remember trying to learn how to inhale the smoke by pulling tiny puffs down my throat. I was coughing and sputtering but not giving up until my lungs would allow me to hold down a whole puff.

I knew it was the wrong thing to do. But right then, with those first few pulls off those cigarettes, I made a bad choice that would lead to an addiction to tobacco—a habit I would be afflicted with for fifteen years.

Almost all of the detrimental things I've ever gotten involved with started with baby steps. Little, seemingly insignificant choices can bloom into full-blown problems unless you make a conscious and committed effort to nip them in the bud.

Bad choices come with consequences, and so many times I went against the voice that was telling me not to make the choice I did. Lies, fights, taking advantage of a weaker person, and many other things I've done that I'm not proud of, all ended with me paying a price in pain, regret, and worst of all, remorse. Not to mention all the other, more tangible penalties.

Taking the time to consider long-term ramifications can save you a lot of future heartache. Listen to that little voice inside of you; it won't steer you wrong.

Choices are like crossroads. Once you pick a path, you have to go down it for a ways before you can turn around and change directions.

LET'S ALL
MAKE THE DAY
COUNT.

43

INVESTING YOUR TALENT

"I was afraid, and went and hid
your talent in the ground."
—MATTHEW 25:25 NKJV

I f I am asked advice about succeeding in a profession, I always preface it by advising to choose a profession you love, something you can put your heart into.

Sometimes, going into the family business or pursuing a profession your parents want you to go into can have disastrous results and make for an unfulfilling experience. Although your parents mean well and have your very best interest at heart, nobody can live your life for you. Finding yourself strapped down to a job you hate is no way to spend life.

I believe that everybody has a talent for something. When we ignore that talent and choose a profession to please some-body else or for financial stability alone, we are doing what the unfaithful servant in Matthew 25 did. We are hiding the talent we were given, never giving it a chance to blossom or take root. We're left to wonder for the rest of our lives, *What could I have accomplished if I had only followed my dream?*

———————————————

Sometimes a little boldness is in order. Sometimes thinking outside the envelope, or even shredding the envelope, is also in order.

———————————————

LET'S ALL
MAKE THE DAY
COUNT.

44

HURTFUL WORDS

A soft answer turns away wrath,
but a harsh word stirs up anger.
—PROVERBS 15:1 NKJV

Many years ago while doing a radio interview, I said something about a band that would be on a future show with us.

It was not mean, condescending, or in any way disparaging, but still not as complimentary as it could have been. And it was certainly not meant as criticism or even judgment, as I had never even heard the band play.

Their name simply came up in the course of the interview, and I made a very bland statement basically saying that I was not familiar with them.

One of the band members was listening and took what I said as a bit of an insult. I ran into him years after the incident and he brought it up. He recalled it word for word and the offhand remark I had made was still a distasteful memory.

So many old adages are based in truth, and "if you can't say something good about somebody, it's best to say nothing at all" is one of them.

Words are powerful and can't be unspoken; choose carefully the ones you use.

LET'S ALL
MAKE THE DAY
COUNT.

45

OUR ATTITUDES

Making the most of your time,
because the days are evil.
—EPHESIANS 5:16 NASB

Over the years I have come to the conclusion that much of the outcomes of our lives are controlled by our attitudes—the half-full or half-empty glass, the acceptance of responsibility for our own well-being, willingness to blame our problems on outside influences.

I know, of course, things will happen that are beyond our control, but so much of our lives are within our own ability to affect. What we do with our God-given talent, how we face the problems we are confronted with, and how we choose to view each new day is up to us. Is it just another twenty-four-hour period? Or is it another opportunity, another chance to move forward—a reason to rejoice?

Do we allow ourselves to start thinking that, no matter

what we do, no matter how hard we try, things will never get any better and we may as well save our efforts?

Nothing could be further from the truth. Start out the day being thankful that our Creator has granted another day of life. You are His unique creation, and He has something better for you. Then put aside all the negative thoughts you've been thinking and start looking for it.

How we choose to perceive things, thinking for ourselves, making a conscious choice to look at all sides of a situation before we judge it, trying to approach life with a positive attitude, having patience and understanding can all make such an incredible difference.

Positive or negative, it's your choice.

Every breath is a blessing, every heartbeat a godsend, and every day an act of God's grace.

LET'S ALL
MAKE THE DAY
COUNT.

46

SELF-CONFIDENCE VERSUS CONCEIT

*Therefore let him who thinks he stands
take heed that he does not fall.*
—1 CORINTHIANS 10:12 NASB

Self-confidence and conceit are two different things. Self-confidence is the assurance that through talent, experience, familiarity, and ability you can handle a certain situation or perform a certain task.

Conceit is many times a false confidence based on competitiveness, braggadocio, and bluster that when put to an actual test, often falls far short of the mark. Conceit can lead the tongue to write a check the mind and body can't cash.

Self-confidence is short on talk and long on action; conceit is the antithesis.

Self-confidence gladly shares the credit, while conceit wants it all.

A self-confident person is content with just being one of the crowd. A conceited person wants to be the center of attention.

Self-confidence is patient, fastidious, meticulous, and takes the time to develop a plan of action that stands the best chance of succeeding.

Conceit rushes blindly forward, impatient and careless, more concerned about being first and leaves many details unaddressed.

Self-confidence is humble and takes success in stride.

Conceit is self-aggrandizing and wants to be recognized.

True self-confidence is gained by being honest about the amount of talent God gave you, knowing your limits and boundaries, and willingly accepting the outcomes.

Conceit never acknowledges boundaries and limitations.

Humility and honest effort go hand in hand with progress.

LET'S ALL
MAKE THE DAY
COUNT.

47

DEATH AND TAXES

"Render to Caesar the things that are Caesar's,
and to God the things that are God's."
—MATTHEW 22:21 ESV

If I looked these United States of America over from coast to coast and border to border, I seriously doubt if I'd find too many people who love to pay taxes, and even less who agree with how our elected government spends them.

But whether we like it or not, taxes are a way of life. It is the price of living in civilization and being able to turn on a tap for our water rather than having to go to a well or a spring every time we get thirsty. It is the price for having law enforcement that keeps the jungle at bay.

There is nothing wrong with using every loophole, legal dodge, write-off, or deduction we can to pay less taxes. That's the law. But when we go past that stage, when we actually cheat, we are not getting back at the government; we are stealing. Period.

There was a time in my young life when I was working a regular job in the daytime and playing in a band at night. I was paid in cash for my band job and didn't file the money, thinking the government wouldn't notice. After all, I was paying taxes on my day job.

Big mistake!

I am here to tell you that the IRS did notice. I had to pay every back cent I owed in addition to enduring regular visits by IRS agents, which is an intimidating experience.

I have beaten my head against some very hard walls.

Take what is yours, no more,
no less, and live in peace.

LET'S ALL
MAKE THE DAY
COUNT.

48

TIME WAITS FOR NO MAN

Teach us to number our days,
that we may gain a heart of wisdom.
—PSALM 90:12

I remember my mother used to wake me up to get ready for school and then leave for work; whereupon, I'd crawl back in bed and go back to sleep until I heard the school bus go past our house. Then I'd drag myself out of bed, get ready, and hitch a ride to school—three miles up the road—to start my school day by being late for class.

Needless to say, I overcame that proclivity when I entered the real world, where nobody gets you out of bed and being late carries stiffer penalties than bad grades.

The club owners I worked for in the early stages of my career frowned on starting the first set of music late, as their customers may just get up and go down the street to an establishment where the music starts on time.

I developed a very healthy respect for punctuality, and it became a way of life for me. I refuse to waste somebody's time by being late for an appointment. And I expect the same from others. Barring some unavoidable glitch, our organization runs on time, and our shows start right on the minute. Anything less would be disrespectful to the people who bought the tickets.

Life is too short and time is too limited to waste either one.

*Time is rationed. When it's gone,
we will not be issued more.*

LET'S ALL
MAKE THE DAY
COUNT.

THOUGHTS ON WINNING

But godliness with contentment is great gain,
for we brought nothing into the world, and
we cannot take anything out of the world.
—1 TIMOTHY 6:6–7 ESV

There are different levels of winning. There is first place with all the acclamation and accolade, the thrill of being proclaimed the best, and being at the top of the heap for a while. But you don't always have to come in first to be a winner.

Now, I'm not saying that you shouldn't always give it your best and to try with everything that's in you. But there will always be those especially gifted people who will take the top spot most of the time.

So what does winning really mean to you?

Does it represent bragging rights for a season? Or a trophy

that is owned by very few? Maybe a day in the sunshine of being a celebrity? How about being able to prove your true worth to those who doubted you?

I experienced all these emotions in my younger years and had a lot of wins, with the accolade and acclaim that went with it. But I discovered what I really wanted out of my career was longevity and the means to keep the people I had gathered around me through the years steadily and gainfully employed. And I aimed steadfastly in that direction.

God, as He has so many times before, granted me the desire of my heart. Here I am, still going down the road after forty-five years surrounded by my beloved friends and employees.

You aren't likely to see our name at the top of the charts, but we're still out here doing what we love. And in my book, that's a win.

The man who gets what he wants
is successful, but the man who
wants what he gets is happy.

LET'S ALL
MAKE THE DAY
COUNT.

———— *50* ————

INCREMENTS

Do not despise these small beginnings,
for the LORD rejoices to see the work begin.
—ZECHARIAH 4:10 NLT

How many stories have you heard about a mega business that somebody started in their garage, with a pushcart, or just in their homes, beginning with nothing more than an idea? It might be a gap in the marketplace that needs filling, a way of delivering goods that nobody has thought about, or just a way of improving a product or a service.

I remember when I first formed the band, we didn't have the equipment we needed. There were no amplifiers, instruments, road cases, or transportation.

Our record company rented us two vans—one for equipment and one for people. We had no air conditioning and no way of stretching out, except to lie on the floor.

But it still beat a car and a trailer.

We played through amplifiers that squeaked and

squawked and broke down from time to time. One night a band member sat down in the wrong place and turned the only fiddle I had into splinters.

But believing that we had something unique to offer, we kept going. We were always conscious of doing a good show, writing and recording songs, slowly building a following, and little by little being able to get the caliber of equipment and transportation we needed.

It has been many years since those days. But they were the foundation for invaluable experience, battles won, and staying the course.

Small beginnings are the seeds for better things to come.

Never laugh at someone with an obsession and a radical idea, no matter how humble his circumstances. One day you could well be asking him or her for a job.

LET'S ALL
MAKE THE DAY
COUNT.

THE HOLY LAND

"I will bless those who bless you,
and whoever curses you I will curse;
and all peoples on earth
will be blessed through you."
—GENESIS 12:3

The history of the rebirth of the nation of Israel is one of the most amazing stories of the past many centuries. The mere fact that it exists today is a true testament that God still has His hand on His people.

Isaiah 66:8 asks, "Can a country be born in a day or a nation be brought forth in a moment?" Israel was indeed born in a day and brought forth in a moment. The day was May 14, 1948. The moment was when the United Nations voted to partition Palestine between the Palestinian Jews and Arabs.

The entire Arab world was up in arms about the rebirth of Israel and set out to destroy the dream and drive the Jews into the sea. That attitude still exists today among many of the nations of the Middle East.

The Jews of Israel fought and won wars against overwhelming odds from its inception, with few and outdated weapons. In 1967, after a war that only lasted six days, the armies of Israel captured and reunited Jerusalem, which is the most hotly contested piece of land on planet Earth.

Possession of Jerusalem will be the point of contention that triggers the last Great War in human history.

Modern-day Israel—its existence, its progress, and its "never again" will to win—should stand as an example to the world of what can be accomplished in the face of overwhelming odds when God is with you.

I had heard that a trip to Israel would change your life, and having gone three times, I can attest that it has been true in my life.

LET'S ALL MAKE THE DAY COUNT.

---- *52* ----

SATISFACTION IN
YOUR LABOR

There is nothing better for a person than that he
should eat and drink and find enjoyment in his toil.
—ECCLESIASTES 2:24 ESV

My daddy once gave me advice about work. He said, "Find something you like to do, because you'll be working more than you're not working."

In his simple way, I think he was telling me that a man needs to enjoy his work because you never really get away from it. Even when you're not working, you're always aware that you'll be going back to work soon. If you dread it, you'll be miserable.

Back in the fifties, when I left Wilmington, North Carolina, with a guitar and a dream, the music business was uncertain at best. You stood or fell based on the amount of people you could attract. There was no safety net.

I knew all this. I'd heard the stories about those who had tried to make a living playing music and had to go back to a regular job. I realized that the competition for the few spots available was fierce. But I knew I'd never be happy doing anything else. Therefore, I accepted the challenges.

I have always been glad that I walked out on that limb in 1958. Since I learned three chords, I never wanted to be anything but a professional musician. The years of pursuit and fulfillment have been an exciting journey and a life-changing blessing from God.

Almost sixty years after the fact, I'd do it all over again.

Working at a job you despise is no way to live your life. Find your niche; it's out there.

LET'S ALL
MAKE THE DAY
COUNT.

——————— 5^3 ———————

SPENDING YOUR
LIFE WITH SOMEONE
YOU LOVE

*Therefore a man shall leave his father
and his mother and hold fast to his wife,
and they shall become one flesh.*
—GENESIS 2:24 ESV

In the olden days, many marriages were arranged by parents. Two people who had never even seen each other were supposed to exchange vows and live happily ever after.

I can't imagine letting someone else choose the woman I'm going to spend the rest of my life with. I can't understand people pledging to love and honor somebody they don't even know or haven't had a chance to sit down with to discuss their likes and dislikes, ambitions, and faith in God.

Marriage is so much more than the physical side of love.

To be successful your bond needs to run much deeper than attraction.

There will be storms to weather, decisions to make, and sacrifices to be made. Some superficial romance or physical attraction alone will simply not weather those storms.

Finding the love of your life is a serious task that requires diligence, good judgment, soul searching, and honesty.

My wife and I are in our fifty-third year of marriage, and I can't imagine my life without her.

Every day is a fresh and new adventure when you share it with the love of your life.

LET'S ALL MAKE THE DAY COUNT.

— 54 —

WORK AND LEISURE

By the seventh day God completed His work
which He had done, and He rested on the seventh
day from all His work which He had done.
—GENESIS 2:2 NASB

If even the Creator of all things rested from His work, surely we mortals should rest from ours.

There was a time in my life when I did not grasp the importance of "downtime." This is a period we set aside to get away from it all—away from your work, your problems, your anxieties, and all the things in your life that keep you from truly relaxing.

So many times, even when we take time away, we go on vacations that require stress over plane and hotel reservations, arriving on time, and hustling to make sure we fit in everything we've planned to do.

We go home bleary-eyed, stressed-out, bone-tired, and wondering why we spent all that money just to wear ourselves out.

I love my profession, so leaving it behind, even for a few days, is extremely hard for me. My working schedule is such that it takes me a few vacation days just to realize that I don't have to be somewhere else tomorrow, settling down, and enjoying the time I've allotted to relax and refresh.

However, over the years, I have learned the value of taking some time away from our busy work lives—to kick our minds into neutral and let the rest of the world roll by without trying to keep up.

Even a machine needs to be shut down for a while.

LET'S ALL MAKE THE DAY COUNT.

55

THE GREATEST NATION

Peace be within your walls
and security within your towers!
—PSALM 122:7 ESV

In the past sixty years, I have had the honor of performing in every state in our union and seeing it in detail by virtue of crisscrossing it so many times in pursuit of my profession. If there is a place on earth that is more beautiful, more distinctive in its geography, more diverse in its population, I have not found it.

This nation has everything—majestic mountain ranges, two oceans, deserts, rivers, lakes, picturesque hamlets, some of the world's greatest cities, dirt roads that go a few miles, and interstate highways that span a continent.

Did you ever taste the gumbo in Lafayette or sample beef brisket slow cooked over a mesquite fire in the Big Bend of Texas or the Brunswick stew in Macon or the burritos in Santa Fe or the Chesapeake Bay crabs in Baltimore or the fried chicken in Mobile?

Did you ever stand on the overlook at El Paso Del Norte and see the lights twinkling clear over into Mexico or watched a paddle wheeler chunkin' down the Mighty Mississippi?

Did you ever wrestle in a big King Salmon from the icy waters of an outback Alaska river or see a herd of mustangs running free across the barren stretches of Nevada or been snowmobiling in pristine Colorado powder?

Did you ever go to Arlington National Cemetery and see the gravestones of the heroes who have shed their life's blood to keep this nation free?

As the song says:
America, America God shed His Grace on thee.
God bless America, my home sweet home.
A nation to cherish, to protect and defend, and to preserve for the generations to come.

LET'S ALL
MAKE THE DAY
COUNT.

56

DIVISION AND DEFEAT

"If a house is divided against itself,
that house cannot stand."
—MARK 3:25

All too often the Congress of the United States reaches a deadlock state. When this happens, absolutely nothing gets done. They become so politically motivated and intractable that they would rather see the nation and its people suffer than to let credit for progress be given to the opposing political party.

I have worked with bands who have separated into cliques and can't even get through a rehearsal without their biases showing.

Marriages come apart for this reason. Longtime friendships fade and wither. Businesses flounder and nations grow weak and impotent. All this happens just because one faction refuses to acknowledge that the other faction could actually have some good ideas, and vice versa.

When you distill this toxic brew, what you salvage is greed, arrogance, revenge, and conceit. All these are attributes of immaturity, blind ideology, and the unwillingness to sacrifice an iota of pride, even for the common good.

Pride, arrogance, and the conviction that your side is always right can lead down some long dark tunnels with no light and no progress at the end for either side.

From time to time we all need a good dose of humility and patience. We all need to be thrown off our high horse and land hard enough to learn to respect other people, their ideas, and their feelings.

LET'S ALL MAKE THE DAY COUNT.

57

FIRST IMPRESSIONS

Man looks on the outward appearance,
but the LORD looks on the heart.
—1 SAMUEL 16:7 ESV

There is an old story in my hometown about a newsboy who sold papers on the street and went to a car dealership one day. He was totally ignored by the sales staff in the belief that waiting on him would just be a waste of time, since he obviously couldn't afford one of their cars.

Well, as it turned out, he really didn't want a car. He wanted a pickup and had no trouble purchasing one from their competitor down the street.

I can't vouch for the validity of the story. Whether true or not, there is a lesson to be learned here about judging people by their outward appearance.

Martin Luther King Jr. said it so well when it comes to judging others—to do so not by the color of their skin, but by the content of their character. The world still suffers from skin-deep and superficial evaluation of human beings without any idea of who they really are, their conscience, their compassion, or even their intentions.

Old and harmful prejudices, superstitions, and refusing to acknowledge that "all men are created equal," skin color, ethnicity, social or financial status notwithstanding, still plague the human race. It's called bigotry, and it's like a cancer eating away at the peace and well-being of society.

The Bible says we will be judged in the same way we judge others. I like to think my best parts are on the inside. I owe it to others to feel the same way about them.

LET'S ALL MAKE THE DAY COUNT.

58

GOD, FAMILY, COUNTRY, AND WORK

You shall eat the fruit of the labor of your hands;
you shall be blessed, and it shall be well with you.
—PSALM 128:2 ESV

I try to set my life goal priorities in this order—God, family, country, and work.

I always want God to come first in all things. Seeing to the well-being of my family is next, followed by my patriotism. Then is my chosen profession, which makes so many of the goals in my life possible.

I believe in charity. I believe in feeding the hungry, clothing the naked, taking care of the widows and orphans, and all the other charitable undertakings that have been pointed out to us by our Creator.

What I do not believe in is for an able-bodied man

finding a way to game the system and collecting a benefit that he is not entitled to.

That's not how it's supposed to be. Man is supposed to work to support himself and his family. When you scam money, just because the system has become so lax that it's easy to do, it is still stealing. You are living off somebody else's labor, and that certainly does not honor God, country, or family.

Profligate entitlement is an unstable and dangerous system. It breeds hereditary poverty and encourages sloth and idle time too often filled with mischief.

The Bible says that if a man don't work, he don't eat.

Charity should be allotted to only those who cannot possibly take care of themselves and their families. Everybody else should work for a living.

LET'S ALL MAKE THE DAY COUNT.

59

MULEHEADED

Do not be like the horse or the mule,
which have no understanding
but must be controlled by bit and bridle
or they will not come to you.
—Psalm 32:9

It is a proven fact that the only way an animal can be trained is by either repetition or trauma, and usually both.

When you watch a good horse trainer work with a colt, many times they have a whip in their hands. They use it to make the colt behave and pay attention to the training lesson, usually doing the same thing over and over until the colt gets the idea and does it on his own.

A good trainer only uses the whip sparingly. He works toward the time when he doesn't have to use it at all, which means that he has taken the colt through his paces so many times, in other words repetition, until the young horse picks up on the idea that if he does what the trainer is asking him to, the trainer won't use the whip.

Animals are unable to reason. They operate on instinct, and when they are being trained, the instinct to do what you want them to do is firmly established in their mental process so they will remember to respond to commands the same way every time. Even though humans have been given the ability to think, reason, and understand, so many of us have to learn just like a dumb animal.

Either by making the same mistakes over and over until we finally get the idea that it just ain't gonna work, or we get our fingers burned so badly that we cease and desist. Some people learn their lessons early in life, and to others, like me, it seems the process goes on and on.

I guess some heads just have thicker shells than others.

A well-trained animal and a well-disciplined human being are a pleasure to be around.

LET'S ALL
MAKE THE DAY
COUNT.

60

TAKE A LOOK

Hear this, O Job; stop and consider
the wondrous works of God.
—JOB 37:14 ESV

There is an old saying about stopping to smell the roses along the way. In our busy lives—in our pursuit of success—we pass by beauty every day without taking the time to appreciate it.

I'm as guilty as anyone. I have been blessed with going to some of the most beautiful places on earth. But often, during my travels, I've been so intent on the task at hand I did not always take the time to really enjoy the beauty surrounding me.

I remember a few years ago when the band was crossing the Canadian border late at night. We stopped in an isolated area of Montana to let the other vehicles catch up. I got off the bus, and there above me was a sky so full of stars—so pristine, so beautiful—it almost took my breath away.

I hadn't seen such a sight since I was a boy—before the

skies above the Eastern seaboard had gotten so clogged with industrial smoke and jet trails. It was beautiful. Such a nostalgic and wondrous sight.

The older I get, the more I appreciate the song of the mockingbird and the whip-poor-will, the patchwork beauty of a grove of hardwood trees in autumn, the smell of lilac blossoms in the early spring, and watching a new calf run and frolic in the joy of just being alive.

We are surrounded by the beauty of God's creation. Slow down and take it in.

LET'S ALL MAKE THE DAY COUNT.

61

SET IN YOUR WAYS

*There is a time for everything, and a season
for every activity under the heavens.*
—ECCLESIASTES 3:1

It took me many years to realize that I am resistant to change. Not when it comes to any number of things that are beneficial to our society, but in my personal life. I hate breaking in a new pair of boots, so I'll wear an old pair until they become so dilapidated they have to be thrown away.

I just despise it when I have to do an upgrade on my phone or computer. The location of the apps get moved around, and at least to me, things seem to hide on the home page. I feel like I need a road map or, more realistically, a visit from my son to get back up to speed again.

I don't care about what model a vehicle is or how many miles it has on it. I am happy with it until it starts causing me trouble, and it's necessary to make a trade. It always seems that they completely redesigned the car, or in my case pickup or

SUV, since the last time I had a new one. The dash has changed, and all the controls, windshield wiper, speed control, interior lighting, and even the gear shift have changed locations and appearances. It has to be learned all over again, which, to me at least, is very irritating. Why can't they just leave them alone?

Most of the folks who work in my band, crew, office, and ranch have been around for decades. Just the thought of making changes there is painful. But occasionally, due to health, family, or some other reason, one of my musicians, or another type of employee, has to leave. But every personnel change has worked out for the best. I've almost always been able to find a replacement that perfectly fits the job. So even old-school, set-in-my-ways me must admit that change can be good.

Come to think of it, I'm always writing new songs and learning new fiddle licks and going new places. But, I still don't like wearing new boots.

Making sure before you make a change is smart, but being sure and still not making a change is foolish.

LET'S ALL MAKE THE DAY COUNT.

62

KEEPING THE FLAME LIT

Jacob served seven years to get Rachel, but they seemed
like only a few days to him because of his love for her.
—GENESIS 29:20

Knowing what you want out of life, the profession you want to pursue, the lifestyle, and the person you want to share it with are some of the most important decisions you'll ever make. These are decisions to be prayed over and made carefully, as they will come with serious commitment, devotion, and fidelity.

When you enter the bonds of holy matrimony, it means that two people become one person. It requires a willingness to adapt and compromise, each partner accepting the little quirks and personality differences of the other. These things should be talked out well before the vows are taken.

When you choose a profession, you should realize that it's going to become a major part of your life, and the many hours you spend at work should be pleasant and fulfilling.

Then, there will be problems to be handled, sacrifices to be made, and the occasional crisis to be dealt with. The wise person realizes they're coming and is prepared to face them down and move forward.

Sharing your blessings with those who are less fortunate is a blessing within itself. Valuing each day and living it to its fullest makes every day an adventure.

Contentment, satisfaction, and fulfillment are the fruits of good choices, well-laid plans, taking advantage of opportunities as they present themselves, and staying excited about living.

Life is a beautiful thing.
Don't waste a day of it.

LET'S ALL MAKE THE DAY COUNT.

63

THE MOUNTAINTOP

*"I am the way and the truth and the life. No
one comes to the Father except through me."*
—JOHN 14:6

We hear a lot these days about diversity, multiculturalism, tolerance, and sexual parity.

America is a diverse nation. People from all over have
come to this land to seek a better life and the freedom and
liberties Americans take for granted.

Multiculturalism has abounded for over two hundred
years. The culture and heritage of immigrants from around
the world is reflected in their names, their speech, and their
social functions.

The Evangeline country of South Louisiana, Little
Italy in New York, Chinatown in San Francisco, and the
Scandinavian enclaves of the upper Midwest, all reflect the
ethnic origins of the people who have settled there and are
sturdy vertebrae in the backbone of America.

And as far as parity in the workplace for the sexes, I do believe there has been a glass ceiling. It has now been partially shattered as capable women take their rightful places as heads of corporations and in the executive suites of major companies.

And while I do not deny that American citizens have the right to practice whatever religion or faith they choose, America was founded on a Judeo-Christian belief system. Therein the real strength of this nation lies.

I don't buy the adage that "all roads lead to the mountaintop." Nobody but God is on the mountaintop, and His Word tells us that there is only one path to where He is. The Lord Jesus Christ.

The day is coming when it will be extremely difficult to hold on to our Christian faith. Prepare for the battle.

LET'S ALL
MAKE THE DAY
COUNT.

---- 64 ----

THE BIGGEST APPLE

If I speak in the tongues of men and of angels, but
have not love, I am a noisy gong or a clanging cymbal.
—1 CORINTHIANS 13:1 ESV

I remember in my very early days, when my mother gave me snacks to share with playmates. I always gave a playmate the biggest apple or the best piece of candy. I don't even remember having to think about it. It was something I just did naturally, though it had to have been taught and emphasized by my parents.

It didn't go unnoticed that when we were playing at their house and their mother gave them goodies to share with me, they always kept the choicest pieces for themselves. But that didn't deter me from giving them special treatment the next time they came to my house.

It just seemed it was something I was supposed to do.

As I grew older and entered the real world of competition and jealousy, I learned that stepping on somebody else to get ahead is viewed as somewhat normal. I had a hard time grasping the fact there were people who would take advantage of me, no matter how well I treated them.

I had a choice. I could be more careful about who I trusted and not allow myself to be put in a volatile situation, or I could become cold and hard and give back just as good as I got.

I chose the former. And yes, I'm still apt to give away the biggest apple.

Kindness can touch the most calloused heart.

LET'S ALL
MAKE THE DAY
COUNT.

65

FACING WORRY

*"Who of you by worrying can add
a single hour to your life?"*
—LUKE 12:25

It seems worry is covered in Velcro. Any time you let it touch you, it wants to stick to you and go along with you wherever you go and take center stage in your thoughts.

Worry is also possessive, insistent, and never happy until it has your full attention to the exclusion of everything else you need to think about.

There was a period of my life when it seemed I was dogged by worry every waking hour. It tried to control every decision I made, every action I took, as well as my relationships and my demeanor.

Worry has to be faced down and revealed for the charlatan it is. Oftentimes, the overwhelming "what ifs" we worry about will never even happen.

Furthermore, you have to separate the things you *can*

control from the things you *can't* control. Act on the first and ignore the latter.

Alcoholics Anonymous has a prayer that I feel applies not only to alcoholics but to everybody.

"Lord give me the serenity to accept the things I cannot change, to change the things I can, and the wisdom to know the difference."

Do the things you can do and leave the things you can't do to God.

LET'S ALL
MAKE THE DAY
COUNT.

66

BEING FAITHFUL

*"One who is faithful in a very little is also
faithful in much, and one who is dishonest
in a very little is also dishonest in much."*
—LUKE 16:10 ESV

Being faithful should never be taken lightly. It involves commitment, determination, and sometimes self-denial.

For more than the last forty years, it has been my responsibility to, among other things, make payroll for twenty-five people every two weeks. I insure the continuance of their employment, provide adequate transportation to get personnel and equipment to the more than one hundred concerts we perform every year, and make sure I'm at the top of my game for every show.

Now I alone can't possibly take care of all these details, so I must delegate responsibility. To delegate well means hiring people you can trust with your money, your career, and, in the case of the drivers who ferry their human cargo thousands of miles a year, your life.

In the early days, I put my dependence in some who were less faithful, less honest, and less trustworthy; I got my fingers burned and became much more selective about who entered into my confidence and trust.

When you delegate responsibility, one weak link in the chain could shut down the whole operation. I have been blessed with capable employees who shoulder the responsibilities assigned to them and get the job done, making them valuable assets.

Accepting responsibility is a covenant of trust—a serious undertaking that can reap great rewards for a worthy person.

LET'S ALL
MAKE THE DAY
COUNT.

67

DEALING WITH BULLIES

Though I walk in the midst of trouble,
you preserve my life;
you stretch out your hand against the wrath of my enemies,
and your right hand delivers me.
—PSALM 138:7 ESV

Every generation has its bullies. When I was young, schoolyard bullying was fairly common. Being an only child, I didn't have an upperclassman sibling who would take up for me, so I was left to fend for myself. Unlike today, the playgrounds were largely unpatrolled and absent any adult supervision. Most bullying incidents were settled with fisticuffs.

Now, before anybody gets the opinion that I'm recommending that present-day problems should be settled by fights, please know that I'm not. That's just the way it was in those days, and I'm actually aiming at a larger lesson here anyway.

It seemed that as much as my family moved around,

being the "new kid" was practically an avocation with me. It seemed that I was constantly being confronted, and it meant either defending myself or becoming a doormat. I chose the first method.

I didn't always win the battles, but most garden-variety bullies don't really want to fight anyway. If you stand up to them every time, win or lose, they soon pass you over when they feel like picking on somebody. The average bully is really a coward. When confronted they back down in a hurry.

Today bullying has gotten to be an even more serious problem than it was in my day, and the results amount to a lot more than a busted lip or a black eye. Bullying should be interdicted by adults at the first sign of trouble. Whatever measures it takes should be employed to either reform the bully or remove them from the general population of children. That's the only way this very serious problem will ever be solved, and it desperately needs to be.

Sometimes fire has to be fought with fire.

LET'S ALL
MAKE THE DAY
COUNT.

68

CHEWING IT UP AND SPITTING IT OUT

Do not be among those who give pledges,
among those who become guarantors for debts.
—PROVERBS 22:26 NASB

There was a time in my career when I was faced with tremendous debt. When I looked at it as a lump sum, it seemed almost insurmountable and threatened to cost me everything I had worked so hard for over many years.

Giving up was one option, but one that never crossed my mind.

I prayed for God's help and sought competent counsel. I let all my creditors know that they would be paid over time. Then we set about removing this burdensome albatross from my neck.

It was one of the most stressful times of my life and seriously increased the amount of show dates we had to play to provide the revenue to clean up the debacle. Vowing to never let it happen again, we went nose to the grindstone and put our hand to the plow.

The debts were a tangled mess, in differing amounts and spread out among many creditors. We paid everything we could on each of them monthly.

We applied the Dave Ramsey method. Any extra money we had at the end of the month was applied to the smallest debt we had until it was paid in full. Then we started on the next smallest debt and repeated the procedure until we were able to burn the paid-off notes in my front yard.

Hallelujah!

A big problem is usually a series of little problems. Study it, separate it into increments, prioritize the increments, and then deal with them.

LET'S ALL
MAKE THE DAY
COUNT.

69

FACE TOMORROW, TOMORROW

"Do not worry about tomorrow, for tomorrow will worry about itself. Each day has enough trouble of its own."
—MATTHEW 6:34

I don't know of anybody who, at one time or another, has not worried about what is going to happen tomorrow.

Of course, we can prepare for it—make plans, arrangements, and reservations, and even organize our thoughts—and we should. But it's totally impossible to live one second of tomorrow until it arrives. Putting so much thought and energy into worrying about it could mean that we leave something we should do today undone.

I have tried to develop a habit where while I'm still lying in bed in the morning, I ask myself, *What do I need to do today?* Then I think through my priorities and prepare for whatever tasks are at hand.

I can tell you from firsthand experience, after you have made all the mental and physical preparation you can to deal with what you have planned for the future, and you've prayed about it and done the best you can, worrying about it is not going to change even one minute detail about what's going to happen tomorrow.

Yesterday's gone and tomorrow has not yet arrived.

Today is upon us; live it as if
it is all you'll ever have.

LET'S ALL
MAKE THE DAY
COUNT.

70

THE LITTLE THINGS

"It is like a mustard seed, which is the smallest
of all seeds on earth. Yet when planted, it grows
and becomes the largest of all garden plants."
—MARK 4:31–32

It's easy to get caught up in the grand scheme of what you're trying to accomplish. And it's hard to dwell on the often mundane and boring tasks of first doing the groundwork and laying the foundation.

You might leave very important, but little, tasks inadequately done because they appear to be inconsequential. But such tiny details can cause structural damage. Typically, the little things don't grab our attention until we roll out our grand idea, only to find that it has to be repaired.

In my case, it can be writing a song and leaving a section of weak chord structure or a meaningless line of lyric. So when I think I've finished the song, I have to go back and make it right, necessitating the entire remake of that part of the song. It's kind of like having to tear down a whole section of wall to replace one bad brick.

Being meticulous can be tedious, but it sure makes a difference in the long run.

Tie up the little loose ends as you go. Then when you finish, you're truly finished.

LET'S ALL
MAKE THE DAY
COUNT.

71

SELF-CONTROL

Better a patient person than a warrior,
one with self-control than one who takes a city.
—PROVERBS 16:32

Once in a while, everybody flies off the handle to one degree or another. Maybe they say a few words they regret or do something they feel bad about later; it's just human nature. The rational person makes amends and moves on.

But people who have no control over their temper are truly horrifying. You don't know how they are going to react in any given situation. They wear their feelings on their sleeves and rage is always close to the surface. They rant and rave, accomplishing absolutely nothing except making everybody else feel miserable.

You reach the point that you don't even want to be around those people because dissension and unpleasantness follows them around like an unfed puppy. When we allow our tempers to get away from us, we plant bitter seeds and will reap a harvest of resentment and hard feelings.

Taming a temper is like training a wild animal. You have to take control and be vigilant. It will turn on you and overwhelm you and become even more unmanageable every time you let it have its way.

Tempers have to be dealt with at the first sign of arousal, before their temperature gets too hot to handle.

Control your temper, or
it will control you.

LET'S ALL
MAKE THE DAY
COUNT.

72

ADMIT DEFEAT

Whoever tries to hide his sins will not succeed,
but the one who confesses his sins and leaves
them behind will find mercy.
—PROVERBS 28:13 THE VOICE

One of the hardest things for some of us to do is to admit to ourselves that we have faults. We will go to all kinds of lengths to blame our shortcomings on another person, an outside influence, our health, or any number of erroneous trivialities just to continue our charade.

Before I finally admitted to myself in 1968 that I either had to stop smoking or face serious health problems, I blamed my perpetual colds, lung infections, and shortness of breath on germs and contagions. I was eventually forced to face the fact that these side effects were caused by the four packs of cigarettes I was inhaling each day.

Similarly, early on in my music career, I would blame my lackluster playing on the poor quality of the instrument or the deplorable shape it was in. And my lack of energy in school was never the consequence of the simple fact that I stayed up late the night before and didn't get enough sleep.

Blaming your faults on other people and other things can become a habit that turns you into an irresponsible liar that nobody trusts. It's best to deal with it.

Admitting your faults is the only way to correct and overcome them, and it's a sign of maturity and character.

LET'S ALL
MAKE THE DAY
COUNT.

73

TRUE FRIENDS

Love is patient, love is kind. It does not
envy, it does not boast, it is not proud.
—1 CORINTHIANS 13:4

What is a friend?

I know what a friend means to me.

A friend is someone you can trust in every situation; someone who always gives you the benefit of the doubt; someone who is willing to drop everything and come running when you need them.

A friend is someone you can share your innermost secrets with; someone who always has your back; someone who neither judges nor condemns you, but is completely honest in giving even the harshest opinions.

A friend will never betray or forsake you.

A friend is someone who deserves the same loyalty and consideration they devote to you.

True friendship is priceless and reciprocal, a two-way

street, a covenant of trust and fidelity, a relationship that always goes the extra mile and cannot stand if ignored or violated.

True friends are rare and precious and should be treated and valued as such.

LET'S ALL
MAKE THE DAY
COUNT.

74

TENACITY PLUS PERSEVERANCE EQUALS PROGRESS

The end of something is better than the
beginning. Patience is better than pride.
—ECCLESIASTES 7:8 GNT

I had a horrific accident in 1980 involving farm machinery. It resulted in three compound fractures in my right arm that basically immobilized me for four months.

After my arm healed enough for me to resume some activities, I found that I was in such a deteriorated state that I could barely walk one hundred yards without being totally out of breath. I knew this wouldn't do, so I set out to do something about it—knowing it was going to take patience and regimen, both of which were fairly foreign to me at the time. However, I increased my daily walk by a few steps a day until I was covering a decent distance. Then I increased my pace until I was jogging two miles a day.

It was a slow and laborious process that tested my will and determination. But I stayed with it, and it all worked out for the best. Even when I did regain most of my physical health, I found that my right hand and arm were so stiff that my guitar neck felt almost like a board. The only answer was to tackle it straight ahead and spend a lot of time practicing scales to loosen my fingers up.

Now I hate running scales. It's repetitive and boring, but I learned its value during that time of my life and still play scales as part of my musical fitness regimen.

I realized the importance of regular exercise in my life and have maintained some form of daily exercise ever since, but it all started with those first one hundred yards.

Difficult trials can be overcome by continuously placing one foot in front of the other and proceeding in the proper direction.

LET'S ALL MAKE THE DAY COUNT.

75

LOOK IN THE MIRROR

For each will have to bear his own load.
—GALATIANS 6:5 ESV

Have you ever worked with people who wouldn't carry their part of the load, do their fair share of the work, or pull their own weight?

They never help put up the tools, clean up the workplace, or do any of the extracurricular duties that go along with doing a job well. As soon as the clock strikes quitting time, they're out the door, and they have the habit of showing up to work five to ten minutes late most mornings.

They complain about everything. Nothing is their fault. They don't like the boss. They don't get paid enough. They think they get singled out for all the hardest jobs, and they never volunteer for anything.

These are the people who will always populate the bottom rungs of the ladder, who will do just enough to get by, limp through the job, and never understand why everybody else moves on while they never move an inch.

These are not necessarily bad people. They have just fallen into the trap of thinking that all the powers of the world are aligned against them. Somewhere along the line, whether it was the way they were raised or they were influenced in some other way, they never put out any extra. They've developed a victim attitude, and it permeates every thought and every action.

It's an easy snare to get caught in. All it takes is a little self-pity, listening to dissatisfied people, and forgetting that the reason you've got a job is to make a profit for the company you work for. The reason things sell for different prices is that some things are worth more than others. Employees are the same way. If you want to get ahead, make yourself more valuable; and if you want somebody to help you, look at the guy in the mirror.

Feeling sorry for someone else is a virtue; feeling sorry for yourself is a waste of time.

LET'S ALL MAKE THE DAY COUNT.

76

RECIPROCITY

"Do unto others as you would
have others do unto you."
—LUKE 6:31 MEV

As implistic, non-academic way to define the word *reciprocity* would be "you get back what you put out." In biblical terms, we reap what we sow.

People who continually sow discord spend their lives in constant conflict with one person or one group or another. Many times they are arguing about something that, in the true scheme of things, doesn't amount to a hill of beans.

Those who take themselves too seriously in thinking they're several rungs up the professional and societal ladder, to the point of arrogance and condescension, many times find themselves having to eat humble pie at the table of someone they had belittled who has climbed past them on the success scale.

There were bands we opened shows for in the early days

that treated us badly, which some artists seem to think is supposed to be standard procedure. Later on down the line, fortunes would change. They would be opening for us, but we always treated them fairly.

And I've had it work the other way. Bands that once opened shows for us went on to a bigger headline status, and we were opening for them. They always remembered how well we had treated them and were always considerate.

Being civil and caring is a conscious decision. It just requires a modicum of humility and consideration and remembering that there is a law of reciprocity.

What goes around comes around, but it comes around harder and faster and leaves more damage behind.

LET'S ALL MAKE THE DAY COUNT.

77

WISDOM AND
KNOWLEDGE

Let the wise hear and increase in learning,
and the one who understands obtain guidance.
—PROVERBS 1:5 ESV

When I was very young, getting a college degree was
looked upon as a way to assure a good job and a bright
future.

Not as many high school graduates went to college
because college was expensive, and the scholarship opportunities were not as plentiful. Most of the ones who did go
majored in fields where qualified workers were needed and
did benefit from their education.

But nowadays, with government programs and numerous
scholarship opportunities, almost anybody who wants to can
get a higher education. Unfortunately, so many of them are
majoring in obscure fields where employment opportunities

are limited or nonexistent. All the diplomas they receive represent is several years out of their lives.

Please don't misunderstand me; I believe in education. But how many philosophy majors can the workplace absorb? Why doesn't whoever is helping them decide what to study realize that? Why end up with a degree that's good for nothing except hanging in a frame on the wall? It's a sad thing to see an overeducated young person clerking in a grocery store or flipping burgers.

Knowledge is one thing. Wisdom and common sense are another. They work well together.

LET'S ALL
MAKE THE DAY
COUNT.

78

SPITE AND PETULANCE

"But to what shall I liken this generation?
It is like children sitting in the marketplaces
and calling to their companions."
—MATTHEW 11:16 NKJV

Spite is usually meant to hurt somebody else, and petulance is just a way of trying to make somebody feel sorry for you. Neither one works in the real world.

I've had employees who have timed their leaving the band to cause inconvenience and disruption, and the only inconvenience or disruption they've caused is to themselves. I simply replaced them and carried on as if they'd never been there at all.

Nobody wants to deal with a petulant, childish, irresponsible employee who can't be depended on. With these types of individuals there's always something wrong and never of their making. Such people finally reach the point that they are not worth keeping around, no matter how good they are at their job. Their perpetual state of agitation affects those they work with and causes dissension and bad attitudes.

They usually fall by the wayside, and the world just walks around them. It's a shame to see a talented person become more trouble than they're worth.

If you think everybody else should treat you special, one of these days you're going to walk off the cliff of reality, and it's a long, long fall.

LET'S ALL MAKE THE DAY COUNT.

79

COURSE CORRECTIONS

Apply your heart to discipline
and your ears to words of knowledge.
—PROVERBS 23:12 AMP

I am the kind of person who hates dissention, unpleasant situations, and harsh words, and I try to avoid such scenarios whenever it's possible. However, being responsible for the well-being of twenty-five other people, it becomes necessary for me to reel in an out-of-bounds employee once in a great while or settle an argument between two individuals who see things differently.

I dislike this part of my job, but sometimes I am forced to take some action. I try to do it as unobtrusively as possible. Unless the situation makes it impossible, I do it in private, do not raise my voice, and have learned never to discipline an employee while I'm angry.

Traveling on the road in a band means a group of people living in close proximity. In the case of traveling on a bus within a few feet of one another for hours at a time, it takes some common courtesy and consideration. Most of my disciplinary conversations deal with personality clashes and disagreements.

I seldom have to get involved, but my employees know that when I do I'm serious. I've only terminated a handful of people over the more than forty-five-year history of the band. I like to handle things on the practical side when possible.

There are few things more aggravating than a busload of musicians with a long way to go, sitting and waiting on a tardy band member. I instituted a rule on the band and crew bus many years ago. There is a fifteen-minute grace period from the announced time of departure. If you don't make it or you don't let somebody know that you've got a very good excuse for being late, the bus drives away without you. Then it's your responsibility to get to the next show at your own expense.

Worked like a charm.

Better a little bit of discipline now than a whole lot of trouble down the road.

LET'S ALL MAKE THE DAY COUNT.

80

STICKING TO IT

But whoever keeps his word, in him
truly the love of God is perfected.
—1 JOHN 2:5 ESV

There are some people we don't expect to keep their word. Politicians are known for making promises they have no intention of keeping, and there are acquaintances who have broken their word to us so often that we don't trust them anymore.

There are companies who make promises about the products they sell. And it's only after buying them that we find out we've spent our money on a piece of junk.

As one who has broken promises and not lived up to my word many times in my life, I am a witness to the fact that your word, your honor, and your reputation are among the most valuable possessions you'll ever have.

And once lost, they are among the hardest to get back. Rebuilding trust is an extremely difficult task. It requires a contrite spirit, a willingness to admit when you're wrong, and a meticulous devotion to always telling the truth, no matter what.

I learned my lesson the hard way long ago. If I give you my word or make you a promise, you can depend on me doing everything in my power to make it happen.

Your reputation precedes you, but it also goes behind you. It doesn't amount to much if you don't make good on your word.

LET'S ALL
MAKE THE DAY
COUNT.

81

A Mile in My Shoes

"Why do you look at the speck of sawdust
in your brother's eye and pay no attention
to the plank in your own eye?"
—LUKE 6:41

Most all of us have 20/20 vision when it comes to seeing the faults of other people. But our eyesight deteriorates significantly when we look in the mirror.

There have been so many times in my life when I have drawn a quick and critical assessment of somebody, only to find out later on that there was a very good reason for that person to be the way they are. There was a sickness, a bad experience, or some personal tragedy that had literally altered the course of their lives and made them bitter, morose, or maybe fatalistic.

There are combat veterans who have experienced first-hand the death of their comrades or lived in constant danger for so long that the unhealed scars go deep. Those of us who have never been there can never understand.

And how can the uninitiated understand the pain of a Gold Star Mother, a child that nobody wanted, or a derelict alcoholic who has lost all hope. There are reasons for people being the way that they are. Many times, they are so traumatic and personal a person can't find a way of sharing them, even with the best-intentioned folks they come in contact with.

I learned early on, snap judgments can be totally misleading. Until I manage to get this plank out of my eye, I will try hard not to notice the speck of sawdust in somebody else's.

You can't judge the size of an iceberg by its tip. The real problems lie below the waterline.

LET'S ALL
MAKE THE DAY
COUNT.

82

GET IT IN WRITING

*To give a human example, brothers: even
with a man-made covenant, no one annuls
it or adds to it once it has been ratified.*
—GALATIANS 3:15 ESV

The family and circle of friends and acquaintances I was born into and raised with were serious about giving their word. Once they did, they stood by it, whatever the cost. No formal contract was needed. Once a pledge was made, barring death or some other catastrophic occurrence, it was kept to the letter of the covenant.

Of course, those times and those people are long gone. However, there are still a handful of people in my personal circle whose handshake is still as good as gold. Unfortunately, the rest of the world has to be dealt with by formal, meticulously written, airtight documents.

In my early years, when I was struggling to get a foot in the door, I signed some papers I came to regret later on. When there is no money involved, small points are easily overlooked. But later on, if large amounts of money come into play, the small points become huge.

Putting it all on the table and hashing out even the smallest of details before you put your name on the dotted line can save big problems further on down the road.

Work out your differences before you enter into an agreement; otherwise, little things can become big things.

LET'S ALL
MAKE THE DAY
COUNT.

83

CHILDREN ARE A
BIG RESPONSIBILITY

*Train up a child in the way he should go: and
when he is old, he will not depart from it.*
—PROVERBS 22:6 KJV

The upbringing of a child falls squarely on the shoulders of the parents who brought it into the world. When parents shirk that duty and there is no one else to take up the task, chaos usually results.

In this age of political correctness and scientific approach to child raising, the denial of absolutes, and the "let them choose for themselves" attitude prevails. When a child is way too young to know enough about life to be making any but the most basic of decisions, that is, at least in my opinion, no way to raise a child.

My own upbringing required a lot of repetition and a little bit of trauma. In other words, I had to do it until I got it right. And when I got too far out of hand, a modicum of corporal punishment in the form of a keen switch was meted out.

Corporal punishment is frowned on in so many ways these days and viewed as too harsh. But it has saved a lot of lives when applied with explanation and love.

Spoiled children have a hard time in the real world when they find out that temper tantrums and self-centered attitudes won't get them their way.

Children raised without discipline are likely to remain children all their lives.

LET'S ALL
MAKE THE DAY
COUNT.

84

LIMITED SUPPLY

LORD, remind me how brief my time on earth will be.
Remind me that my days are numbered—
how fleeting my life is.
—PSALM 39:4 NLT

No matter how healthy, no matter how successful, no matter how confident, young, or wise a person may be, there is no way of telling how long he or she will live.

The Bible says that our days are numbered. We are each allotted a certain amount of time, and when it's gone, so are we.

Time is one thing that can't be fabricated or stretched, and it is more precious than any earthly possession we could ever have.

I consider things like arguing over trivial matters, dissention, revenge, jealousy, and allowing anxiety to rule our days to be a waste of precious time. Not that I always live up to the letter of my convictions, but I strive to.

Our efficient use of time can't only be evaluated by the

hours we devote to our work or to noble pursuits of charity and kindness, because resting the mind and body is essential. The importance of spending time with family and friends cannot be overestimated and will never be regretted.

Time never takes a vacation. It's ours to use wisely or waste. It never slows down, and once it goes it is only relived in memories.

Every day is a gift of God, a twenty-four-hour unit of time for us to use as we see fit, that will soon go its way, never to return again. Make good use of it.

LET'S ALL
MAKE THE DAY
COUNT.

85

COOLER HEADS AND COMMON SENSE

Do not be quickly provoked in your spirit,
for anger resides in the lap of fools.
—ECCLESIASTES 7:9

I have never had a hot temper. I've never been quick to anger or fast to react in an assertive fashion, but I've been around some people who listen to their baser instincts and just have to respond to a disagreeable situation in an aggressive way.

I remember an incident back around 1950 when I was playing junior high football for Tileston in Wilmington, North Carolina. The main high school in Wilmington, New Hanover High, was the home of the Wildcats, and they were one of the top football teams in the state that year, knocking over opponents like bowling pins. One night our junior high coach took several of us players to Durham to watch the mighty Wildcats take on the Durham Bulldogs.

We couldn't believe it. The Wildcats lost, and we walked back to the car disappointed to say the least. The coach hadn't arrived yet, and as we stood beside his car on the street, one of the guys with us started making loud and disparaging remarks about Durham and their football team.

A small crowd started gathering, and even though we tried to hush up our loudmouthed buddy, he kept on dishing out the insults. The boys in the Durham crowd started answering back, worked up the nerve to do something more physical, and had thrown one of our guys to the ground. Our coach finally walked up and cooled out the situation.

The point I'm getting at here is that uncontrolled bad tempers and giving in to foolish impulses can create a bad situation not just for the hotheaded but for those who could become collateral damage in the crossfire. I don't know what would have happened if our coach hadn't showed up when he did, but thank God he did.

Approaching a heated situation with a cool head, respect, and a soothing word can save a lot of headaches.

LET'S ALL MAKE THE DAY COUNT.

86

WHO IS IN CHARGE?

*When He imparted weight to the wind and
meted out the waters by measure. When He
set a limit for the rain and a course for the
thunderbolt, then He saw it and declared it;
He established it and also searched it out.*

—JOB 28:25–27 NASB

For the past few decades the subject of global warming
has become a serious topic of discussion around the
world. It is vehemently believed and defended by some, and
disbelieved and ridiculed by others, depending on whose
science you ascribe to.

There are environmental groups who have predicted dire
circumstances for the planet unless immediate steps are taken
to radically reduce the amount of CO^2 we put into the air.
The planet will heat up to the point that the glaciers at the
North Pole would melt, the waters of the Atlantic would rise,
and Manhattan would be covered in several feet of water.

One deadline for this catastrophic event expired several years ago.

Over the past century, the prophecies have gone back and forth between apocalyptic global warming and an ice age. So to cover all contingencies, global warming has been changed to climate change. Now, whether it's drought, blizzard, snow, no snow, deluge, or dust bowl, it can all be blamed on climate change, which is still accredited to global warming.

Now I am all for taking care of the planet. I realize that there are many steps we can take to clean up the air and waters of our world and think it should be a priority to do so.

But I truly believe in my heart that the universal thermostat is and always has been, in the hand of the One who created it. While mankind is able to do much to improve the global environment, he is not going to be the one to destroy it.

God holds not only planet Earth, but the entire universe in His hands. Man is but a grain of sand in a whirlwind.

LET'S ALL MAKE THE DAY COUNT.

$8\,7$

TEAMWORK

Not looking to your own interests but each
of you to the interests of the others.
—PHILIPPIANS 2:4

I found out in my early years as a band leader that the way to get a bunch of musicians to stay together and play together is to hire players who all have a common interest.

This band has been in business for more than forty-five years, makes payroll every two weeks, and nobody, once hired, loses their job for anything less than incompetence or loss of interest. But the job comes with expectations.

I expect everybody to be on time to leave town or going to a show and in their places on the minute for the start of a night's performance.

I expect the sound out front to be good for the audience, and I expect the light cues to be on the mark. When the show is finished, I expect our equipment to be packed away safely in the truck and ready to roll to the next show.

I expect the bus drivers to get everybody to the next stop safely and on time.

In return for what I expect from my employees, I will give them job security, an amiable work environment, a check that won't bounce every two weeks, a sympathetic ear, and a friend you can depend on no matter what comes your way.

It's a two-way street. There's equity on both sides. It's called teamwork, and it sure works well in all endeavors.

If you're not part of the team, you're part of the opposition.

LET'S ALL
MAKE THE DAY
COUNT.

88

PATIENCE AND PEOPLE

Be always humble, gentle, and patient. Show
your love by being tolerant with one another.
—EPHESIANS 4:2 GNT

For many people, myself included, learning to be patient is one of the hardest things in life. A plane that runs late, a slow computer connection, traffic jams, flat tires, or anything that interrupts my planned routine can bring on impatience and anxiety.

I have known some people who have developed their patience to the point that it seems they're able to take whatever comes along in stride, adapt to whatever situation, and when possible, immediately start exploring options to remedy whatever set of circumstances that have caused the setback.

Now these are the kinds of folks you want around when something really goes haywire.

I strive with my impatience, and when I feel that particular dog straining at the leash, I attempt to jerk back hard and hold on. But unless I'm extremely diligent, I will lose the battle.

And here's the conundrum. Diligence takes patience, and patience takes diligence. Oh well, back to the drawing board.

Just remember: in this world things ain't ever going to run on your time.

LET'S ALL
MAKE THE DAY
COUNT.

89

HOPE SPRINGS ETERNAL

You will be secure, because there is hope;
you will look about you and take your rest in safety.
—JOB 11:18

We've all heard the phrase "All hope is gone." It is one of the saddest statements in the English language. It has a finality, a sense of doom, and the implications that everything has failed. Some unpleasant kind of an end is near.

I know there are times when that description of a situation is valid, but so many times it's a premature declaration of surrender.

There are always those who are ready to give up at the first sign of difficulty; those who do not have the vision or the backbone. When they can't see around the first bend in the road, they're ready to call off all bets and go home.

Hope is never gone until every possibility has been exhausted, every string has been pulled, every measure taken, and every effort expended.

There seems to be a benchmark of sorts for many big undertakings that have been sold for bargain basement prices and walked away from. It is that the third party to buy it makes a success of it.

So when it seemed that all hope was gone, it really wasn't. The idea was sound; it just took fresh ideas and financing to reach its potential.

Everything starts with hope. Before dreams are dreamed, before ambitions burn, or the "impossible" is achieved, even before two people fall in love, there is hope. It's the starting point for everything noble we ever do. Never give up hope.

Keep seeking. Keep knocking. Keep hoping.

LET'S ALL
MAKE THE DAY
COUNT.

90

MONEY AND
EVERYTHING ELSE

*"No one can serve two masters, for either he
will hate the one and love the other, or he
will be devoted to one and despise the other.
You cannot serve God and money."*
—MATTHEW 6:24 ESV

You've probably heard the adage "Money is the root of all evil." But the original source of this quote is from the Bible, and that's not what it says. What it actually says is, "Love of money is a root of all kinds of evil" (1 Timothy 6:10). There's a big difference. It's not having money that's evil; it's what you do to get the money and what you do with it after you get it that can become evil.

Great good has been done by people of great wealth—charitable contributions, endowments, and investments in businesses that employ and sustain thousands of workers.

Conversely, there are those who let the pursuit of wealth take over their lives, pervert their morals, and alienate their friends and family. So many people start out just being frugal, wisely putting aside a nest egg to get them through their later years after their earning power has fallen off, telling themselves that they will live in comfort in their old age.

But somewhere along the way frugality morphs into greed, and they can become stingy penny-pinchers. They guard every cent, denying themselves all but the most basic of human needs. Their money does nobody, including themselves, any good. It becomes numbers on a bank account. At their death, it's eaten up by taxes and distributed to the next of kin, some of which the hoarder may not even know.

A hard worker and cheerful giver is
a blessing to all. But a miser who is
willing to gain wealth at the expense of
another's well-being is a curse to himself
and all who have contact with him.

LET'S ALL MAKE THE DAY COUNT.

91

YOU AND YOUR GOD-GIVEN TALENT

*Each of you should use whatever gift you have
received to serve others, as faithful stewards
of God's grace in its various forms.*
—1 Peter 4:10

When the word *gifted* is mentioned, our minds usually turn to the performance or creative arts, singers, musicians, actors, painters, etc. But those definitions don't even scratch the surface of the true meaning and scope of the word.

I believe that our Creator gave everybody a gift for something, and it's our responsibility to identify and pursue it.

To some He gives the gift to lead and others the gift to organize, to negotiate, to practice medicine or law or science, to help people to reason together and settle disputes, and to others the talent to seek out and take care of minute details.

To some He gives the ability to compose classical symphonies, others to raise bumper crops, lay brick walls, the compassion to deal with the infirmed and disabled, the courage to wear a badge and place themselves between the public and those who would harm them.

I can't drive a nail without bending it, saw a board square, or do even the simplest of engine repairs. When I watch a truly talented horseman work with a frisky young colt, I realize that it takes something special that I don't have to do that.

Our God-given talents are diverse and unique, and a lot of satisfaction can be found in finding yours and letting it rip.

We all have a talent of some kind.
Identify it, nurture it, and go for it!

LET'S ALL
MAKE THE DAY
COUNT.

92

A TIME TO CAST AWAY

A time to seek, and a time to lose;
a time to keep, and a time to cast away.
—ECCLESIASTES 3:6 ESV

There's an old country love song that goes, "Holding on with nothing left to hold on to."

Have you ever been there and done that?

I have. I have stood by and watched bits and pieces of my world crumble around me, too complacent or too stubborn to admit it was happening until the damage was done. The last drop of juice had been wrung out leaving nothing but a shriveled pulp.

And when it was all over and I looked back down the trail that brought me to this sorry state of affairs, I realized that there were ample signs along the way to have warned me had I just taken the time to recognize them.

I am a big believer in sticking with something you begin from concept to fruition, but everybody is wrong sometimes.

Once in a while, it's just time to cut bait. It's a wise person who recognizes the signs and salvages whatever is left before there is nothing left to salvage.

There comes a time to let go. It might be a business arrangement, a personal relationship, or even some grandiose idea that you're convinced will be the next big thing. Letting go is never easy, but it's not the end. There's always something else to grab hold of.

Keep your eye on the battle at hand, knowing when to advance and when to retreat.

LET'S ALL
MAKE THE DAY
COUNT.

93

FIRST THINGS FIRST

*But seek first the kingdom of God and his
righteousness, and all these things will be added to you.*
—MATTHEW 6:33 ESV

Sometimes I can be distracted from something important by the most mundane, inconsequential, nit-picking, garden variety piece of trivia. It may be a decision that doesn't have to be made for a month or even something that doesn't affect me or what I'm doing in the slightest.

It's kind of like driving a car and not keeping both eyes on the road, not nearly as dangerous, but you get the point.

I am not a well-organized person to begin with. I have a tendency to throw my clothes on a chair instead of hanging them up, not keeping up with the mileage between oil changes, and almost letting my driver's license expire.

Even when I have an idea, I want to make a note of it before I forget it. Even then, if I'm not really vigilant I'll catch myself staring off into space and trying to remember who the Vols are playing next week.

So it's a struggle, at least for me. I have a feeling I'm not alone, not keeping things first. But I'll keep on trying and maybe one of these days I'll even learn to hang my clothes up.

*Approach your duties in
order of importance.*

LET'S ALL
MAKE THE DAY
COUNT.

94

DECISIONS, DECISIONS

The heart of man plans his way,
but the LORD establishes his steps.
—PROVERBS 16:9 ESV

I have made some spur-of-the-moment decisions that have turned out very well, and I have made some spur-of-the-moment decisions that have turned out to be terrible mistakes.

For instance, in 1967, we made the snap decision to move to Nashville and it turned out to be one of the best moves of our lives.

Conversely, when I decided to go into debt to sustain a business that was basically structurally unsound and unsustainable, I signed my name to large bank loans and assumed mountains of other debt without taking the time to determine the feasibility of what I was doing.

Dealing with the ramifications took me years of hard work and anxiety.

So how do we decide when to act hastily and when not to?

1. What are the risks?
2. What are the rewards?
3. Why am I really doing this?
4. Is this something I can live with if it fails?

In the case of moving to Nashville, I had little to lose. I really had little going on in my career where I was, so the only direction was up.

The bank notes were another story. I should have spent a lot of time considering the risks and rewards. I didn't, and I paid.

If someone says it has to be done today, tread carefully; you could be walking on shaky ground.

LET'S ALL
MAKE THE DAY
COUNT.

95

WATCH YOUR STEP

> *Woe to those who call evil good,*
> *and good evil,*
> *who put darkness for light*
> *and light for darkness,*
> *who put bitter for sweet,*
> *and sweet for bitter.*
> —ISAIAH 5:20

Every time I watch a television newscast, the more I'm convinced the world is going absolutely insane and society is on its way to turning totally upside down.

We now live in a society where it seems the message being communicated is that destroying an unhatched eagle egg is bad, but aborting an unborn child for convenience is good.

Our state and federal governments spend billions of dollars providing food, shelter, education, and medical assistance to people who are committing a crime by even being in this country. Meanwhile, many of the men and women who risked their lives defending it, our veterans, walk the streets in rags, sick, drug addicted, and committing suicide at unprecedented rates.

Our inner cities are dilapidated, crime-ridden, drug-infested war zones, and, yet, we send billions of dollars a year to governments who want to destroy us.

Some climate change apologists live in opulent energy-swilling mansions and fly around the country in fuel-guzzling, carbon-coughing private jets to tell us we should cut back on our energy consumption.

But, with the help of God, there is still an island of sanity in a sea of insanity. There are people who refuse to be blinded by the way of the world, people who have the courage to stand against the surging tide of upside-down morals and inverted priorities.

Stand your ground. You're not alone.

The closest distance between two points is still a straight line. Always has been, always will be.

LET'S ALL MAKE THE DAY COUNT.

96

STANDING YOUR
GROUND

Be on the alert, stand firm in the
faith, act like men, be strong.
—1 CORINTHIANS 16:13 NASB

Have you ever had an unpopular opinion that everybody else disagrees with? Something you felt very strongly about, a question of morality, honor, or justice? Something you know deep down, your common sense and your conscience bear out that you are right, regardless of what everybody else says or thinks?

It can be a lonely position, and you may be chided, laughed at, or even ostracized. But in such instances, it's good to remember one thing: the only person you have to live with, answer for, or give an account for in eternity is the person whose body you inhabit. That person's peace of mind is something you and you alone can protect.

Standing your ground when you know you're right is not always easy, but it's always right.

LET'S ALL
MAKE THE DAY
COUNT.

—
97

DENYING HATE A HOME

Do not think of yourself more highly than you ought,
but rather think of yourself with sober judgment, in
accordance with the faith God has distributed to you.
—ROMANS 12:3

I was born into a segregated, Jim Crow South, where
people of color were viewed as second-class citizens and
were denied the same rights, privileges, and advantages the
white race enjoyed.

A child is not born with racial prejudice and feelings of
superiority; those behaviors are taught. In the society of my
formative years, the roots of these pompous fallacies grew deep
and passed through the generations like congenital bad blood.

I discarded these noxious convictions on my own. I
denounced and abandoned them many years ago when the
truth dawned on me just how blindly and evilly wrong, how
vicious and sad this generational curse of prejudice and repres-
sion was.

The same God made us all and told us to love one another. We'd best heed His word.

Hate has no place in the heart of a reasonable man, and reason has no place in the heart of a hateful man.

LET'S ALL
MAKE THE DAY
COUNT.

98

ANGELS UNAWARES

Be not forgetful to entertain strangers: for thereby
some have entertained angels unawares.
—HEBREWS 13:2 KJV

I n these days of uncertainty, we tend to be suspicious of strangers, and not without justification.

But there was a simpler time when society was more compassionate, or at the very least more tolerant toward people we'd never seen before.

I remember, as a child, when it was perfectly acceptable for an itinerant, or "tramp" as we called them, to go to the back door of a residence and ask for something to eat. They were seldom refused.

And someone broken down by the highway could pretty much depend on somebody coming by and helping them fix whatever was wrong. Or they would give them a ride to a place where they could get help.

Unfortunately, for our well-being, we are forced to live by

the rules society has imposed on us and limit our exposure to those we don't know. But occasionally, we come across a situation where the need is obvious and the risk is minimal. That little voice inside you says, *Help this person.*

Do it gladly, thankful for the situation. You never know who you're helping.

When you reach out your hand to help somebody, you usually touch a heart.

LET'S ALL
MAKE THE DAY
COUNT.

99

FINDING YOU

We have different gifts, according to the grace given us.
—ROMANS 12:6

I t is good appreciating, and even emanating, the good traits of someone you admire and respect, someone who stands out from the crowd and has a certain style and confidence.

But it's when we get so caught up in that person we start trying to be them, taking on their mannerisms, their style of dress, and even trying to address a situation in the way we think they would address it that the problems begin.

In my business, that kind of thing is rampant, as we all have our heroes, especially in our salad days. We try to sing like, play like, and even stand on stage like those we choose to model ourselves after.

Look at all the Elvis impersonators that exist today. Now these guys may make a good living doing what they do, but in most cases the public never even remembers their real names.

But a day will come when you have to let go of their star

and follow your own. You must let your own natural talent take precedent, let your own voice be heard, and let your own personality come out.

God made every one of us different. We have our own face, our own voice, and our own ability to reason without having to take someone else's opinion or model our lives after anyone else.

Each one of us is a unique, one-of-a-kind creation with a purpose to fulfill.

Search diligently until you find yours. It's a wonderful journey.

There ain't nobody else like you.
Take advantage of that fact.

LET'S ALL
MAKE THE DAY
COUNT.

100

PROFIT AND LOSS

"For what does it profit a man to gain the
whole world and forfeit his soul?"
—MARK 8:36 ESV

To me, the Bible verse above is one of the most poignant, practical, and plainspoken in the entire book.

It's a cut-to-the-chase question that sums up so much of Scripture in one sentence. As a stark synopsis of beliefs, morality, faith, and living, it should be the bottom-line guide for every decision we make, every goal we seek, and the way we choose to live our daily lives.

Approaching the end of one's time on earth is the most serious stretch of the path of life we've chosen. We realize that the riches and pleasures of the world mean nothing. It will be our most fervent desire to walk those last few steps with a clear conscience, confident that we have forgiven and that we are forgiven. Nothing else will matter.

Every day we are allotted on this earth is a day we will account for when we stand in eternal judgment. Now is the time to make preparation.

LET'S ALL MAKE THE DAY COUNT.

217

About the Author

From his Dove Award–winning gospel albums to his genre-defining Southern rock anthems and CMA Award–winning country hits, few artists have left a more indelible mark on America's musical landscape than Charlie Daniels. An outspoken patriot, beloved mentor to young artists, and still a road warrior at age eighty-one, Charlie has parlayed his passion for music into a multiplatinum career and a platform to support the military, underprivileged children, and others in need.

ALSO AVAILABLE FROM

CHARLIE
DANIELS

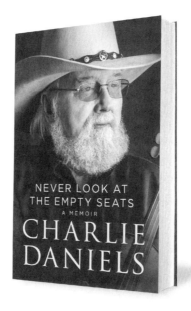

ISBN: 9780718074968

Thomas Nelson
Since 1798

NOTES

NOTES

NOTES

_____

_____

_____

_____

_____

_____

_____

_____

_____

_____

_____

_____

NOTES